# Adult Coloring Book:

# Stress Relieving Designs: Dogs, Cats, Flowers, Mandalas, Horses, and Other Animals (2020 Edition)

By

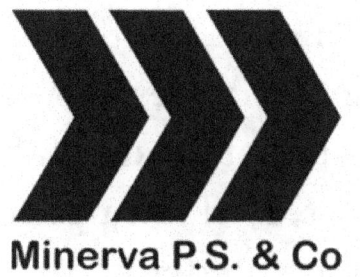

Minerva P.S. & Co

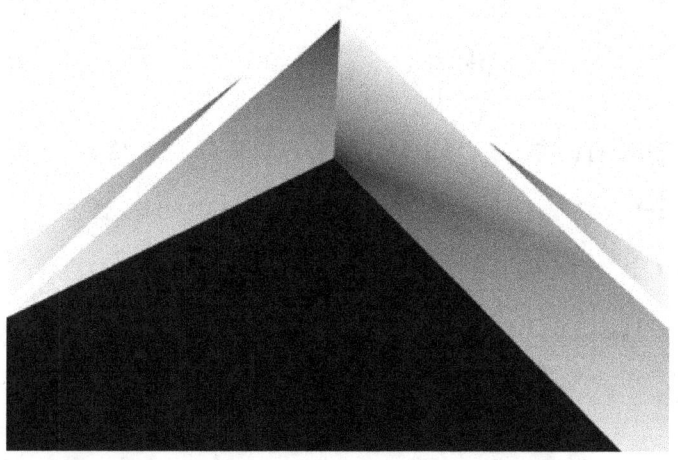

# Copyright Page

**Copyright © 2019 - All rights reserved.**

Under no circumstances will any legal responsibility or blame be held against the publisher for any reparation, damages, or monetary loss due to the information herein, either directly or indirectly.

**Legal Notice:**

This book is copyright protected. This is only for personal use. You cannot amend, distribute, sell, use, quote or paraphrase any part or the content within this book without the consent of the author.

**Disclaimer Notice:**

Please note the information contained within this document is for educational and entertainment purposes only. Every attempt has been made to provide accurate, up to date and reliable complete information. No warranties of any kind are expressed or implied. Readers acknowledge that the author is not engaging in the rendering of legal, financial, medical or professional advice. The content of this book has been derived from various sources. Please consult a licensed professional before attempting any techniques outlined in this book.

By reading this document, the reader agrees that under no circumstances is the author responsible for any losses, direct or indirect, which are incurred as a result of the use of information contained within this document, including, but not limited to, —errors, omissions, or inaccuracies.

# How To Utilize This Book Effectively

Welcome! There are many ways to utilize this book, and we will talk about a few. The designs vary in difficulty for those seeking more to color versus others wanting to tackle more complicated patterns. Coloring is a great way to relieve stress and is a therapeutic tool used by art therapists. Adult coloring books have been becoming more popular, and we are excited to provide pristine illustrations that you can share with your family and friends.

Why is coloring stress relieving? The exact molecular science behind coloring is beyond the premise of this book. However, this question can be answered on a more fundamental cognitive neuroscience approach. Our everyday life is full of highs and lows. We all experience stress and exhaustion. Our minds are constantly focused on tasks and responsibilities. We hardly ever take a step back and let our attentional system rest. The ability to focus is governed by a mechanism involved in cognitive processing. When you color, you will be able to achieve mindfulness. You will be focused on the task at hand rather than obligations contributing to your stress.

Coloring is a great way to bond with anyone! The idea of coloring seems very elementary to an adult. This way of thinking must change because the benefits of coloring have helped many people in their lives. Personally, I was not the biggest fan of coloring. Until one day, I visited my cousin, who has down syndrome, at his daycare. He wanted to color with me, and it felt great. I have always struggled to connect with him because of his condition. I saw what he enjoyed coloring, and I made it into a book (with the help of the best designers, of course)! I hope you guys enjoy the lovely dogs, cats, horses, lions, and elephants.

Coloring is a great tool to use when recovering from a stroke. Life is tough, and acquiring diseases seems inevitable sometimes. Anton Raderscheidt, a famous German painter, suffered a stroke on the right hemisphere of his brain. This led to him developing neglect syndrome, a syndrome characterized by neglection of the left visual field. This is a disorder of attention. Now, Anton kept painting and painting until he recovered all his attention back. Anton proved that by painting or exercising your attentional system, you could increase your chances of recovery. Therefore, it would be a wise choice to try this out if you have suffered from a stroke before.

Lastly, there are many more reasons why one should color. But the most significant benefit of coloring is its mental health aspect. Many people suffer from depression, and this has created a need for pharmaceutical companies to deliver potent drugs to treat it. The era of pharmaceutical agents has led to antibiotic-resistant bacteria and addiction. Research now has shown the side effects of taking drugs to increase serotonin levels, and it is time we focus our attention on other therapies.

For those who are new to our brand, we mostly make books on science. We focus on preventative medicine and figure out ways to prevent diseases. Everyone here in Minerva is excited to create a product that you can utilize every day. I hope you make the best out of these designs, and if you want more, email us. We will be happy to give you more illustrations. You can find our contact information at the end of this book. Thank you for your support. Now, let's grab our colored pencils and color away!

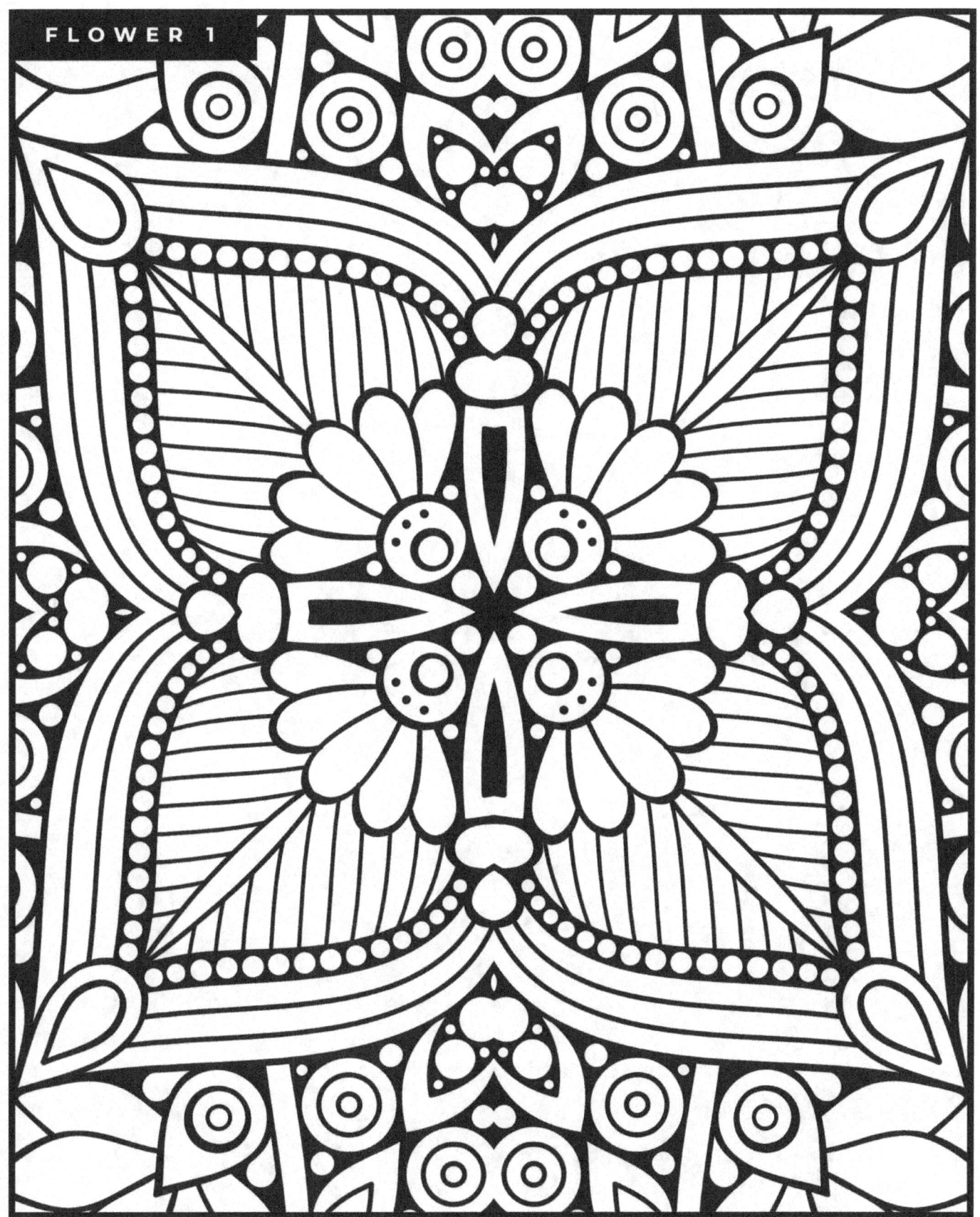

FLOWER 2

FLOWER 3

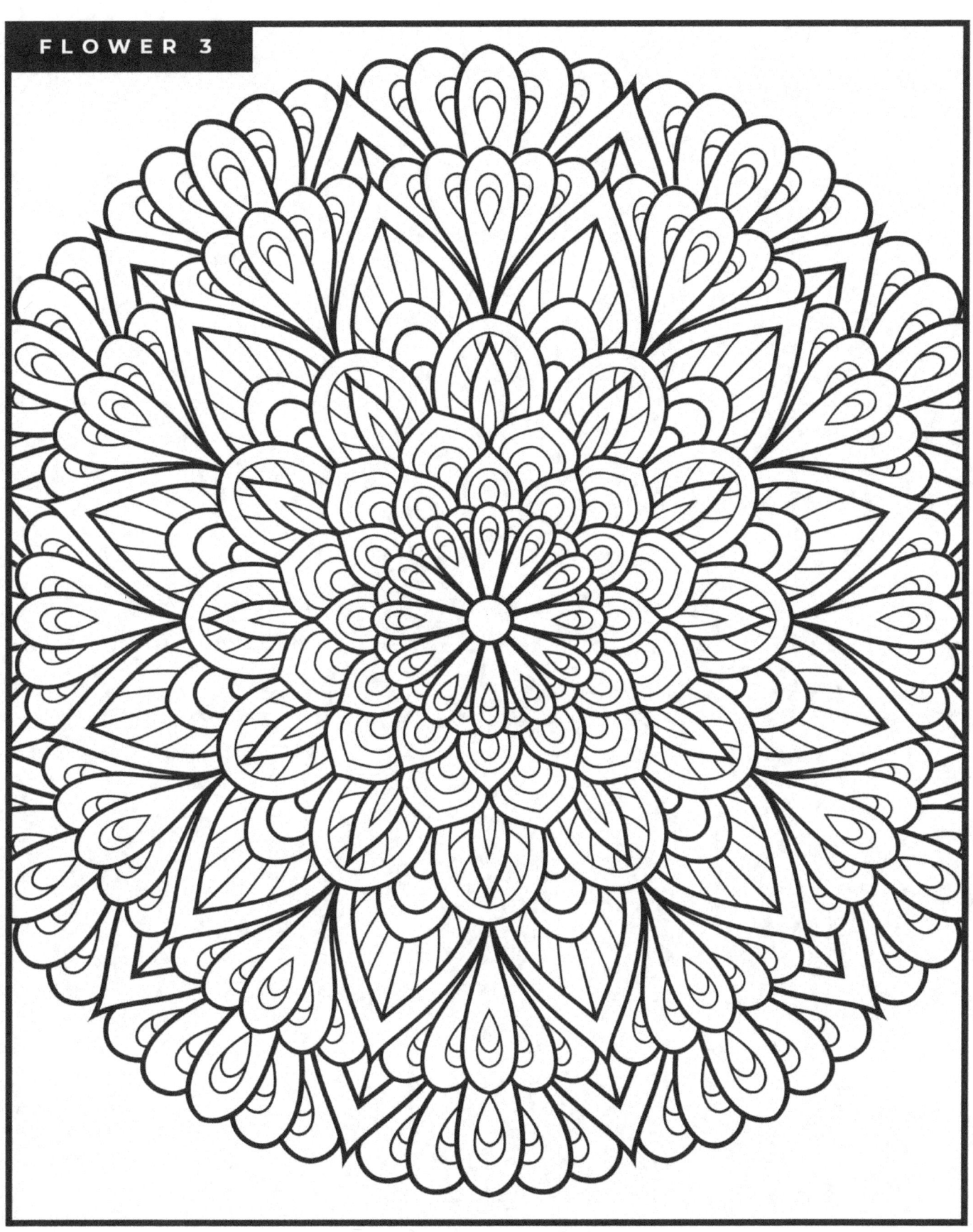

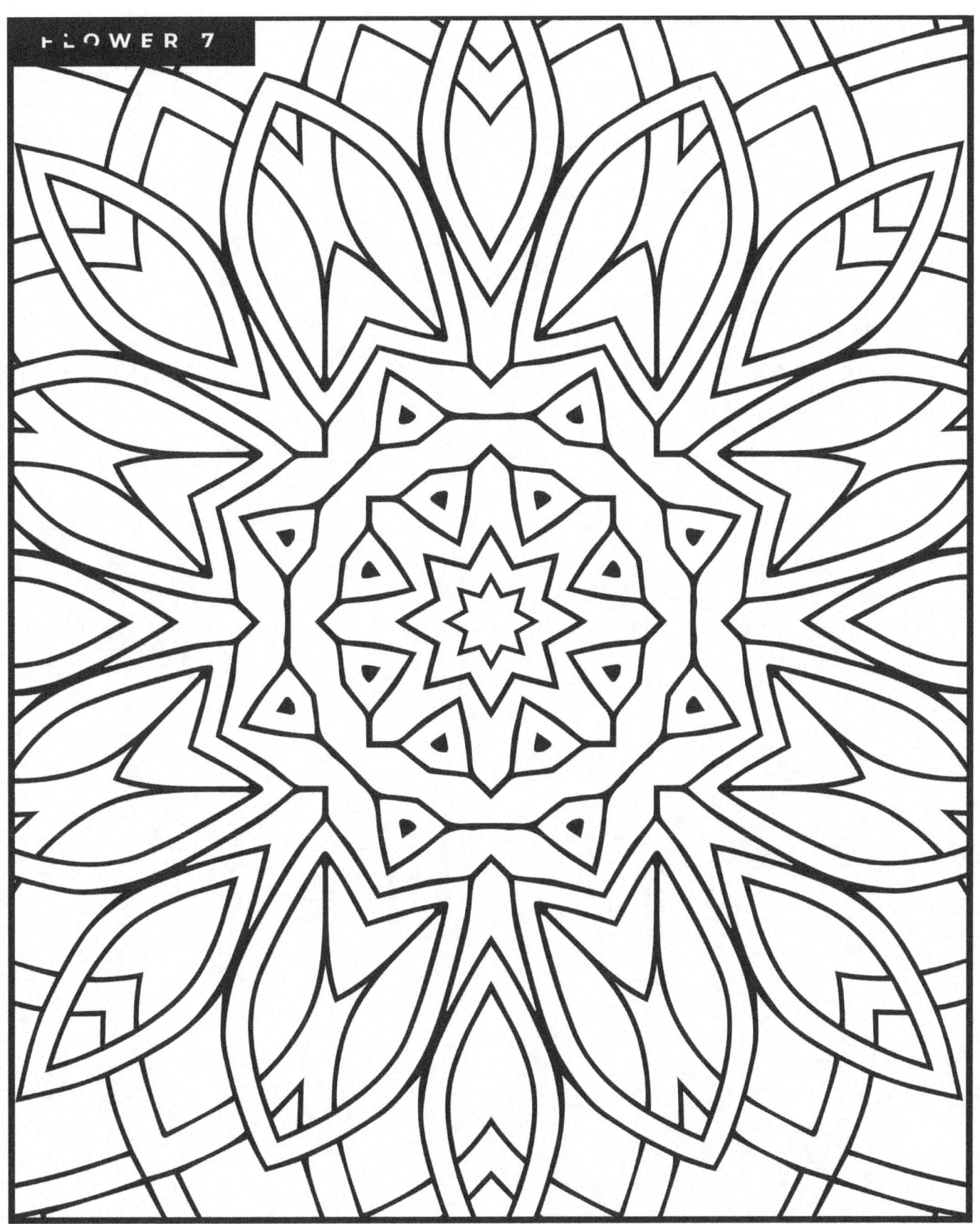

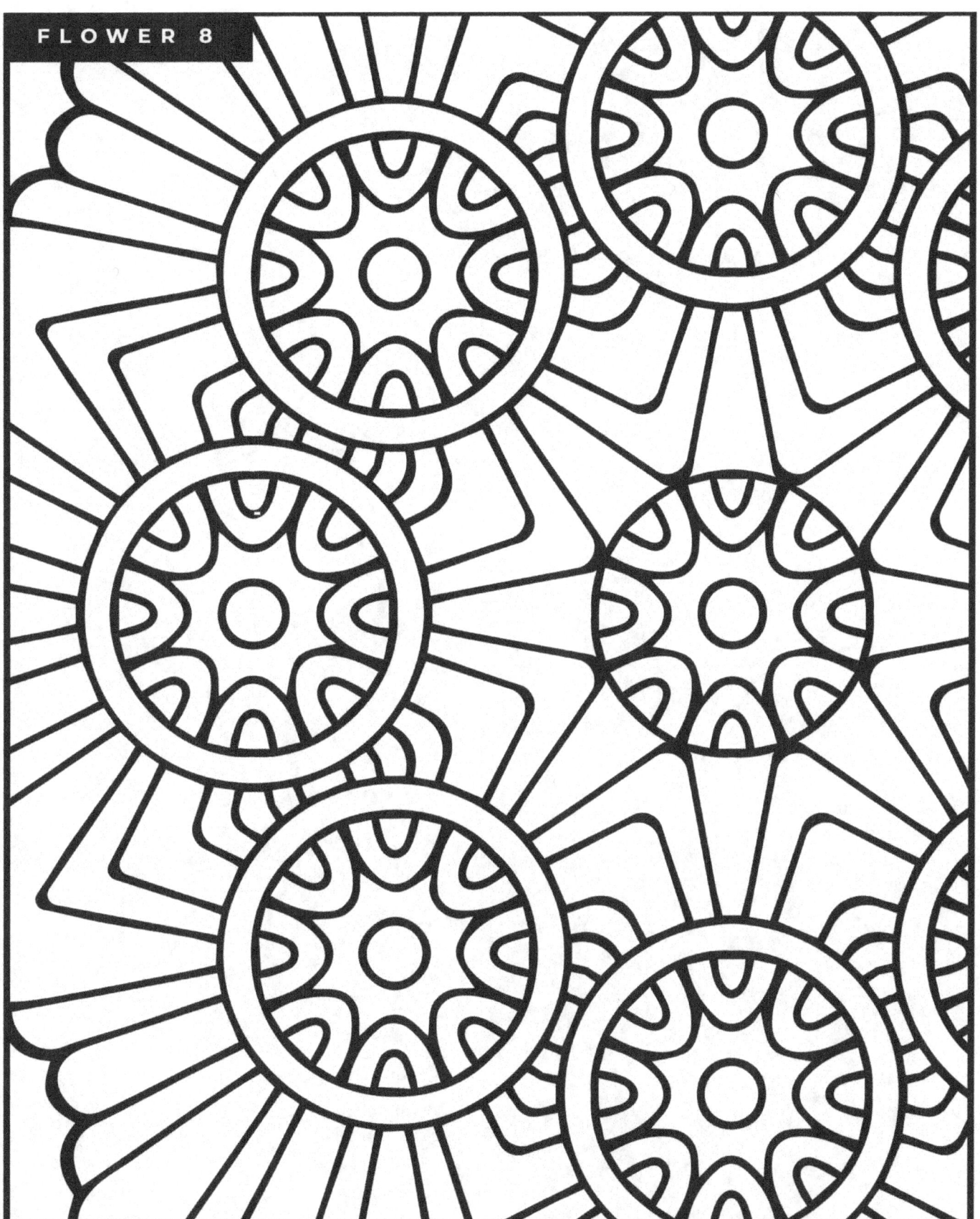

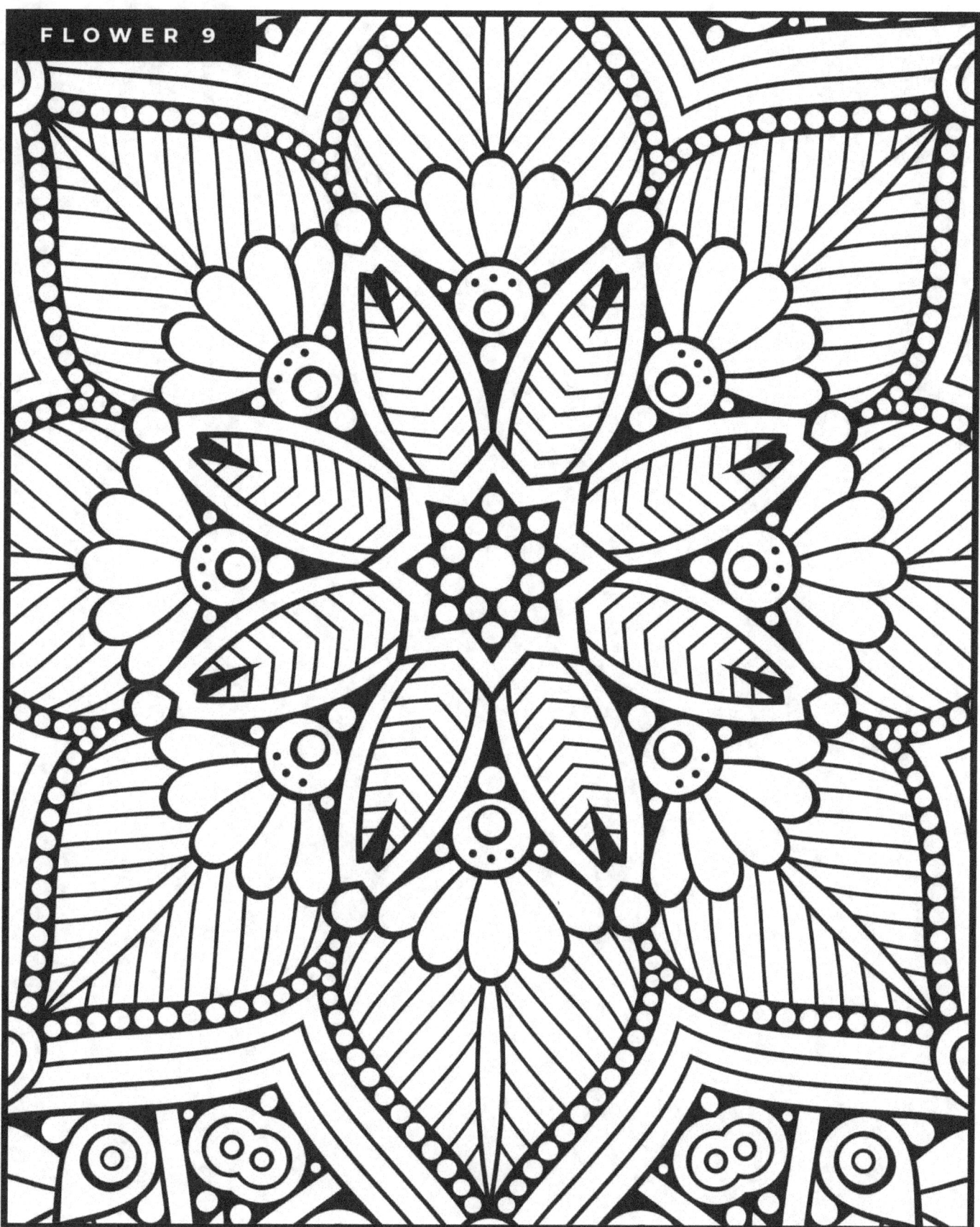

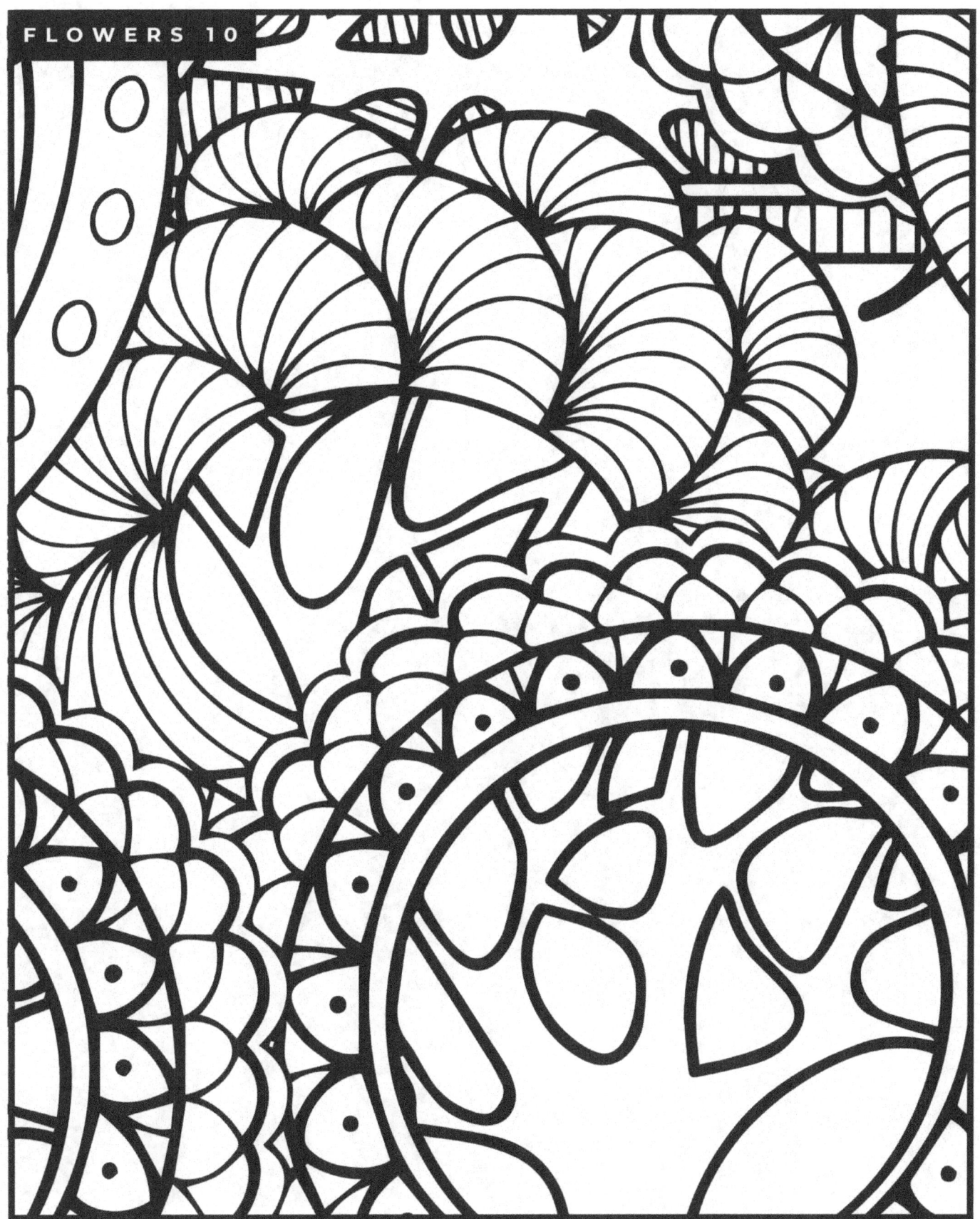

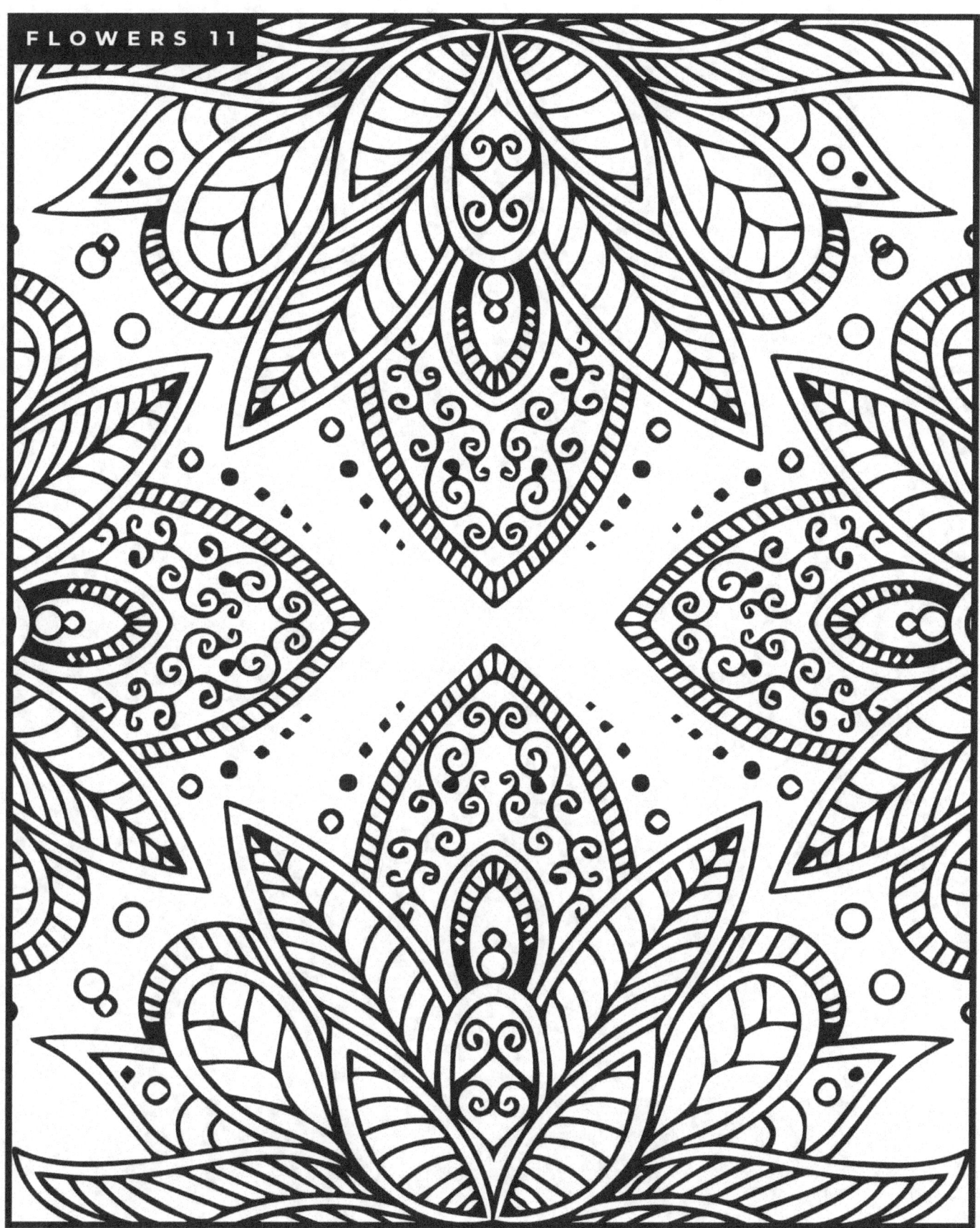

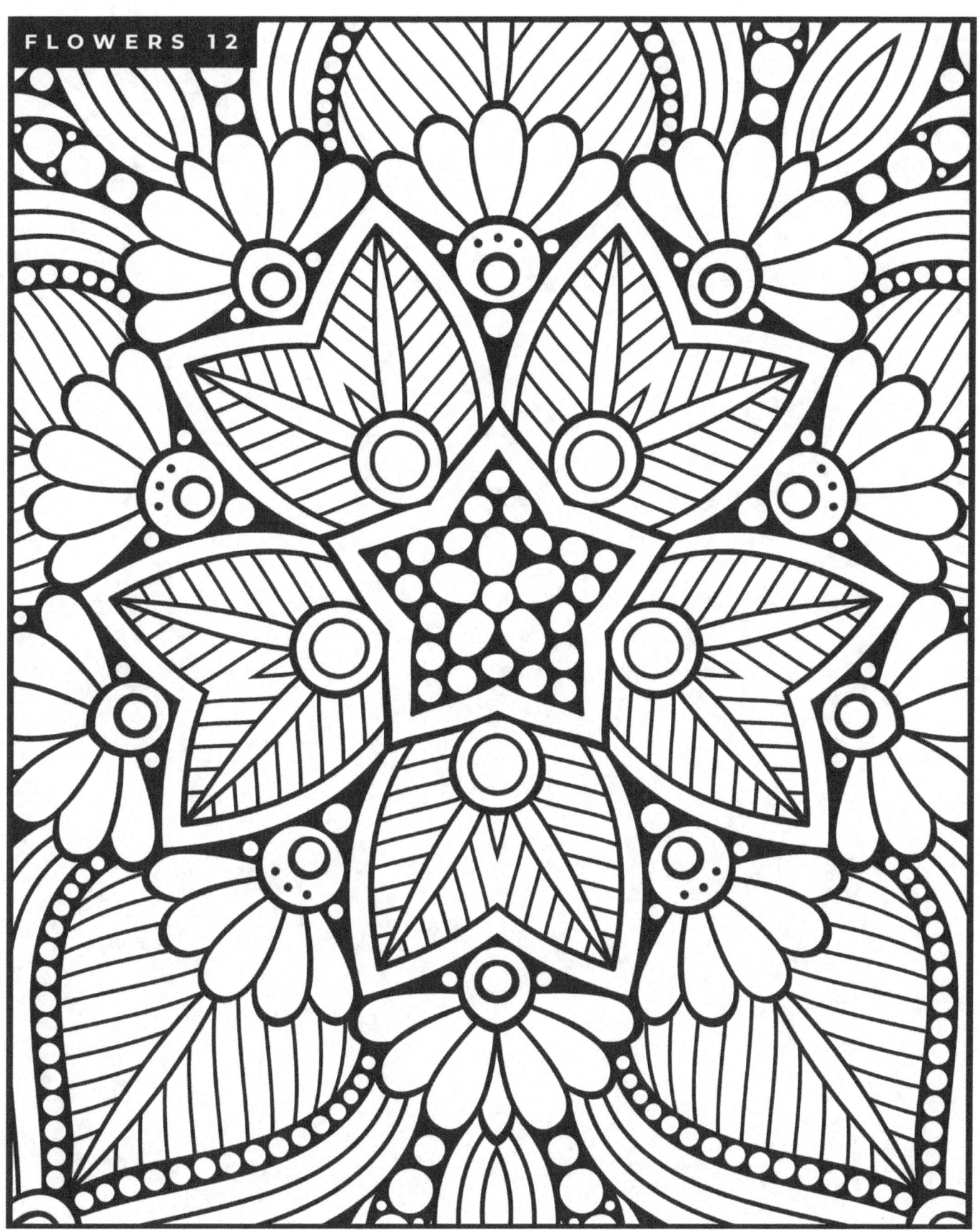

FLOWERS 12

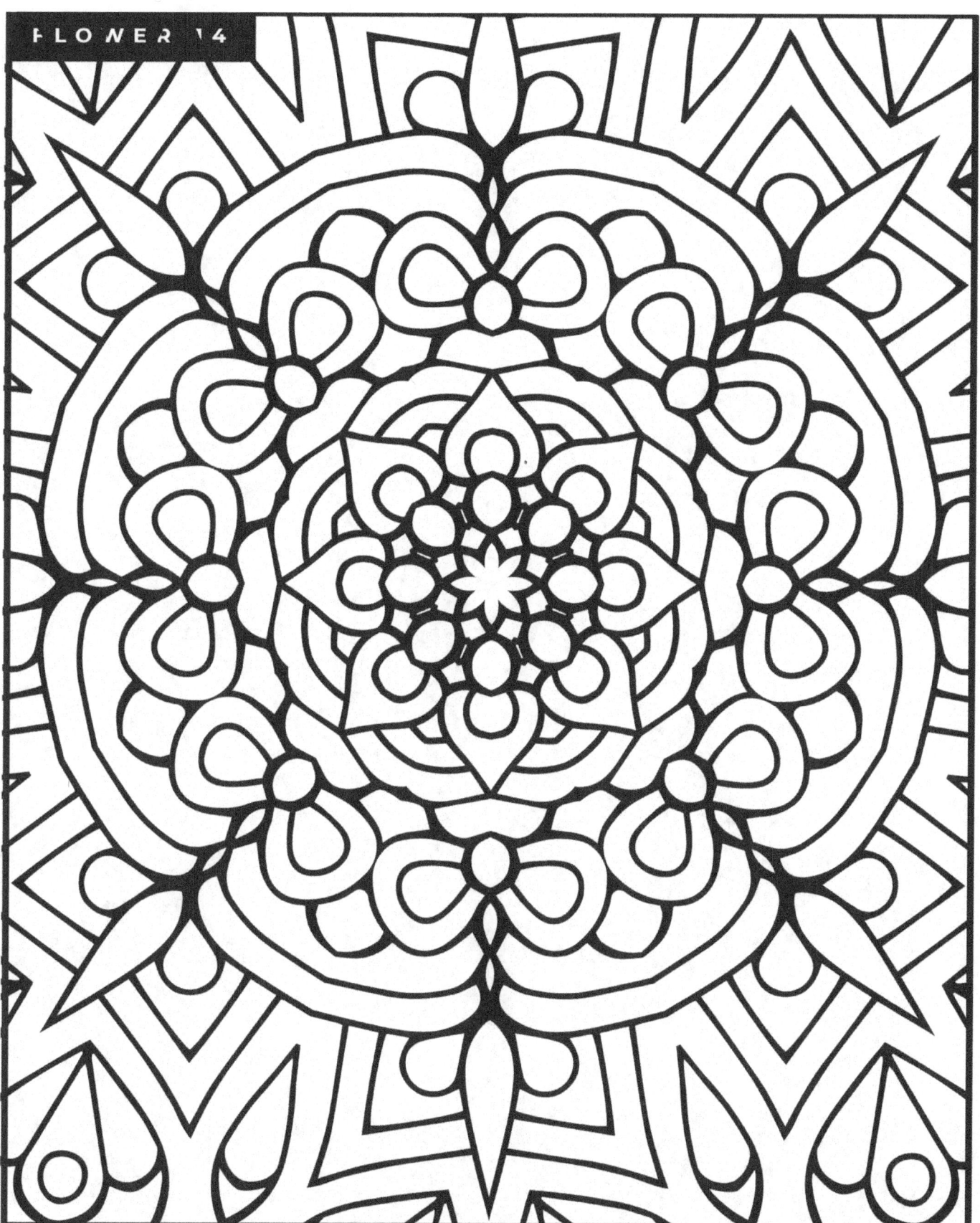

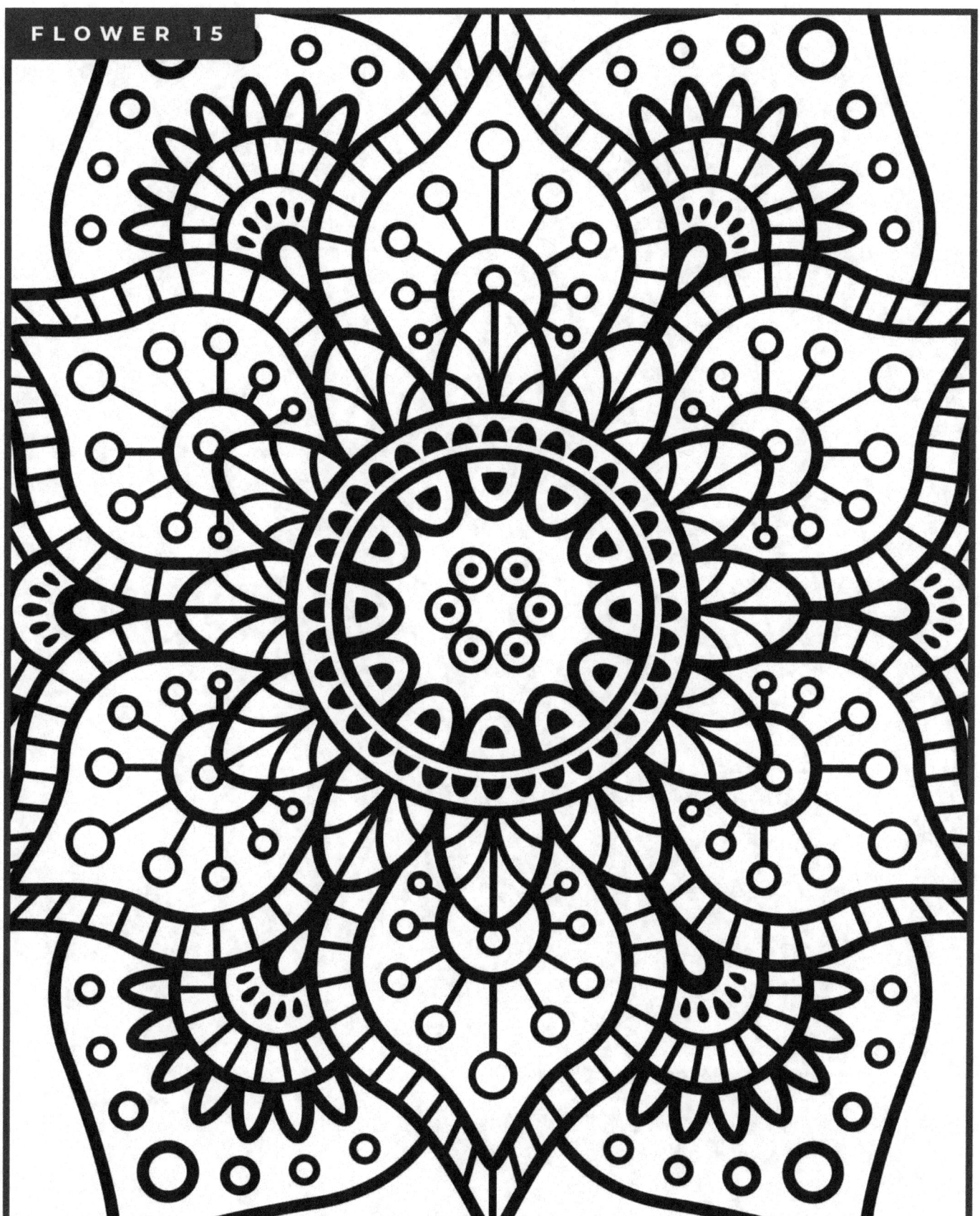

# LION 1

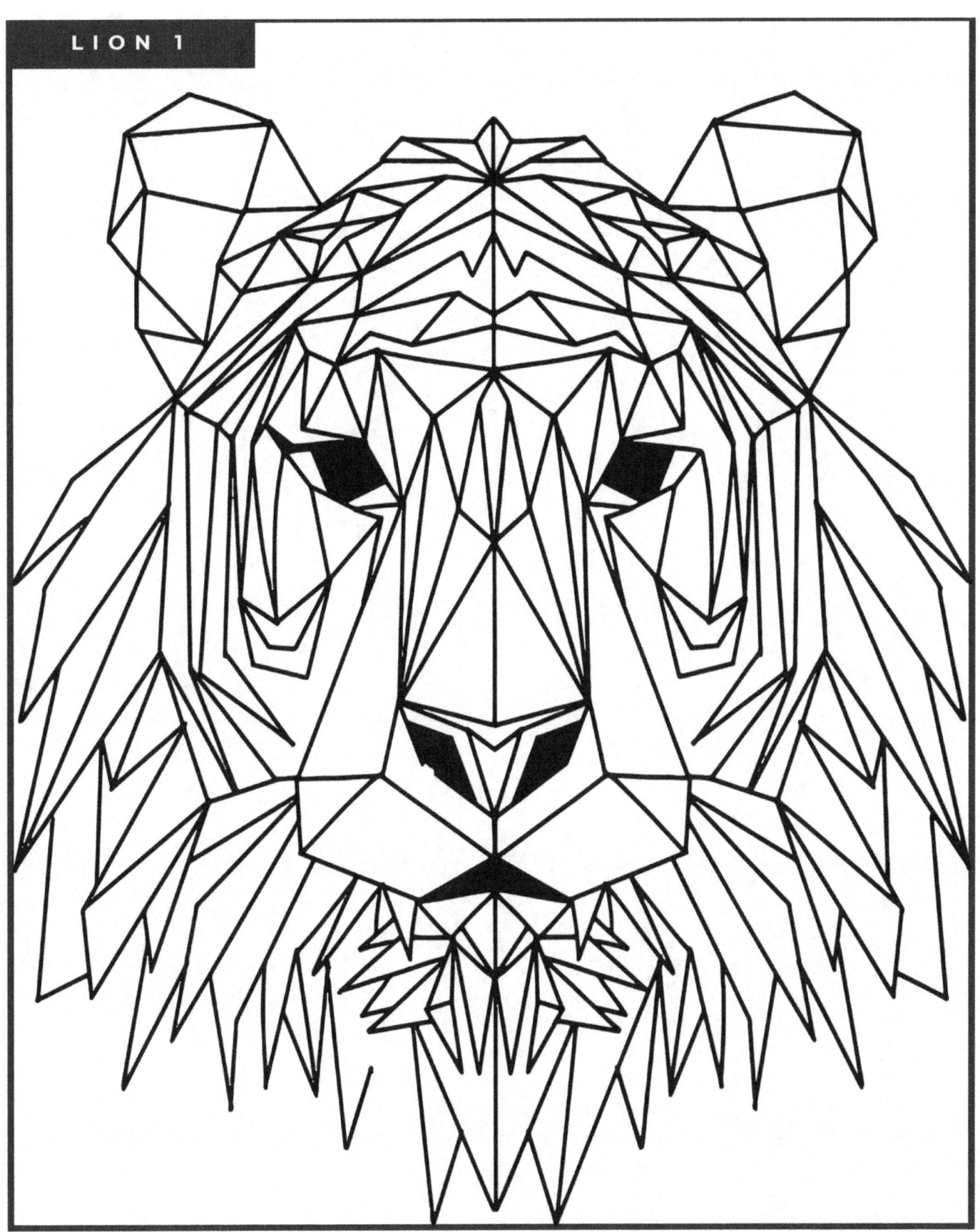

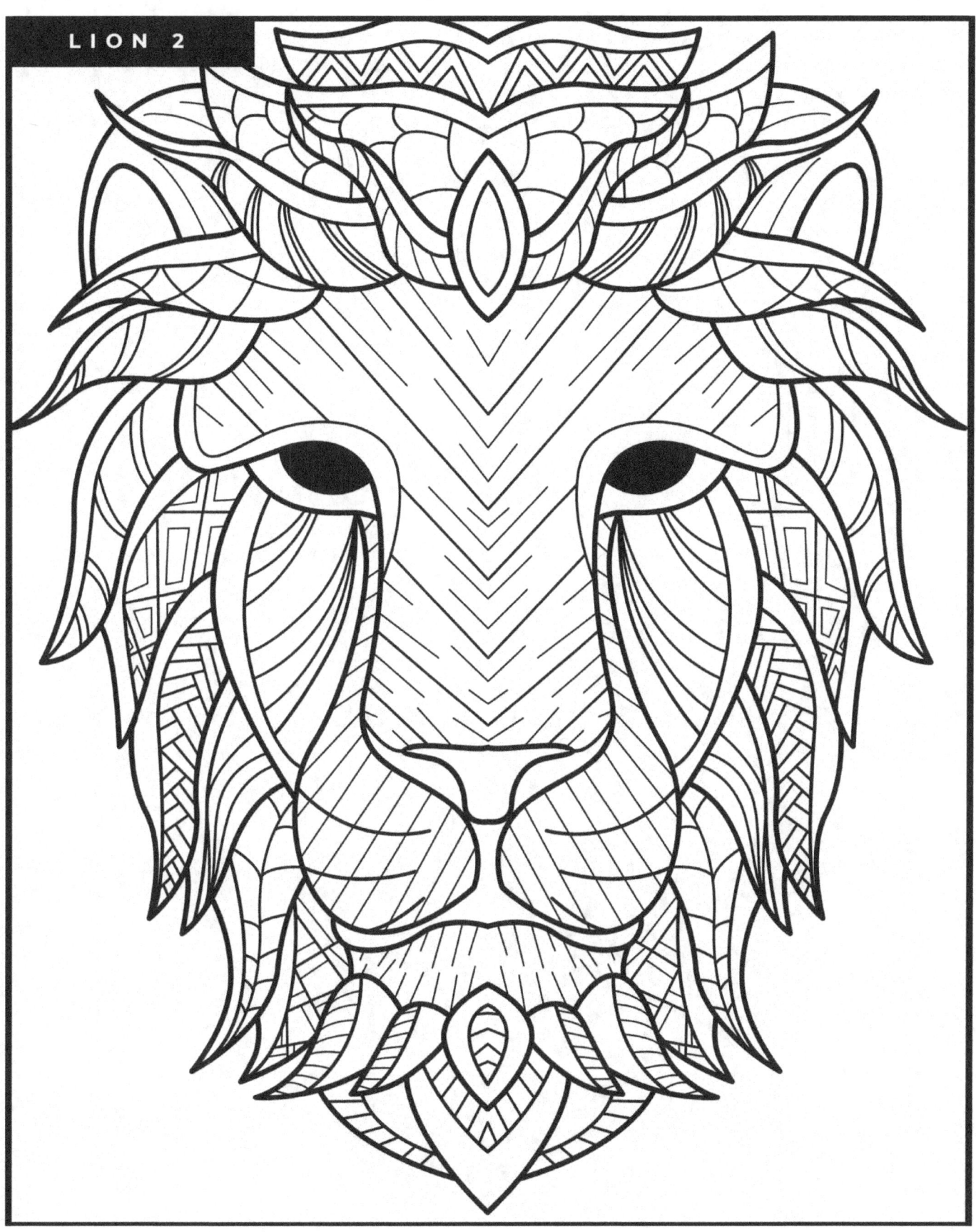

# LION 3

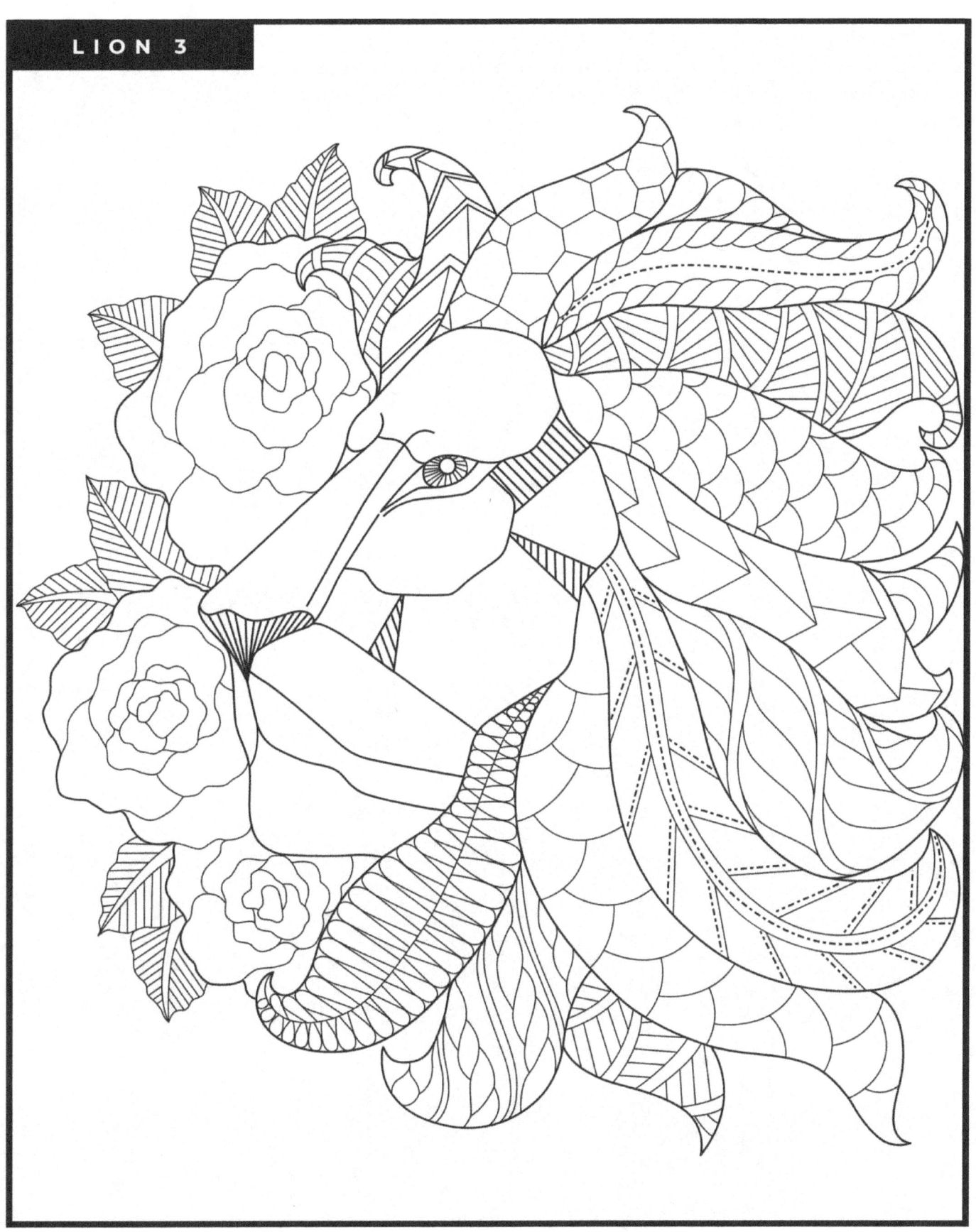

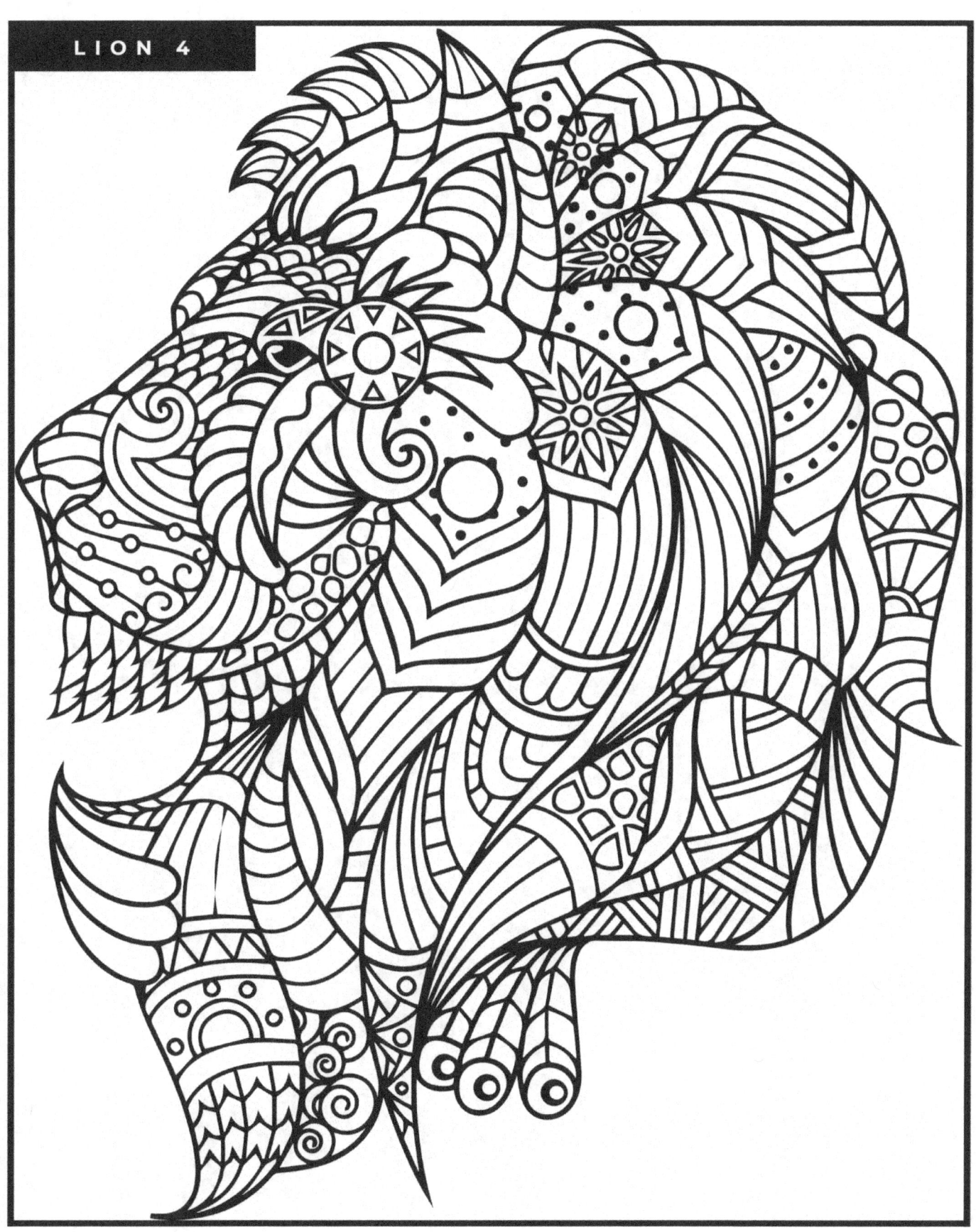

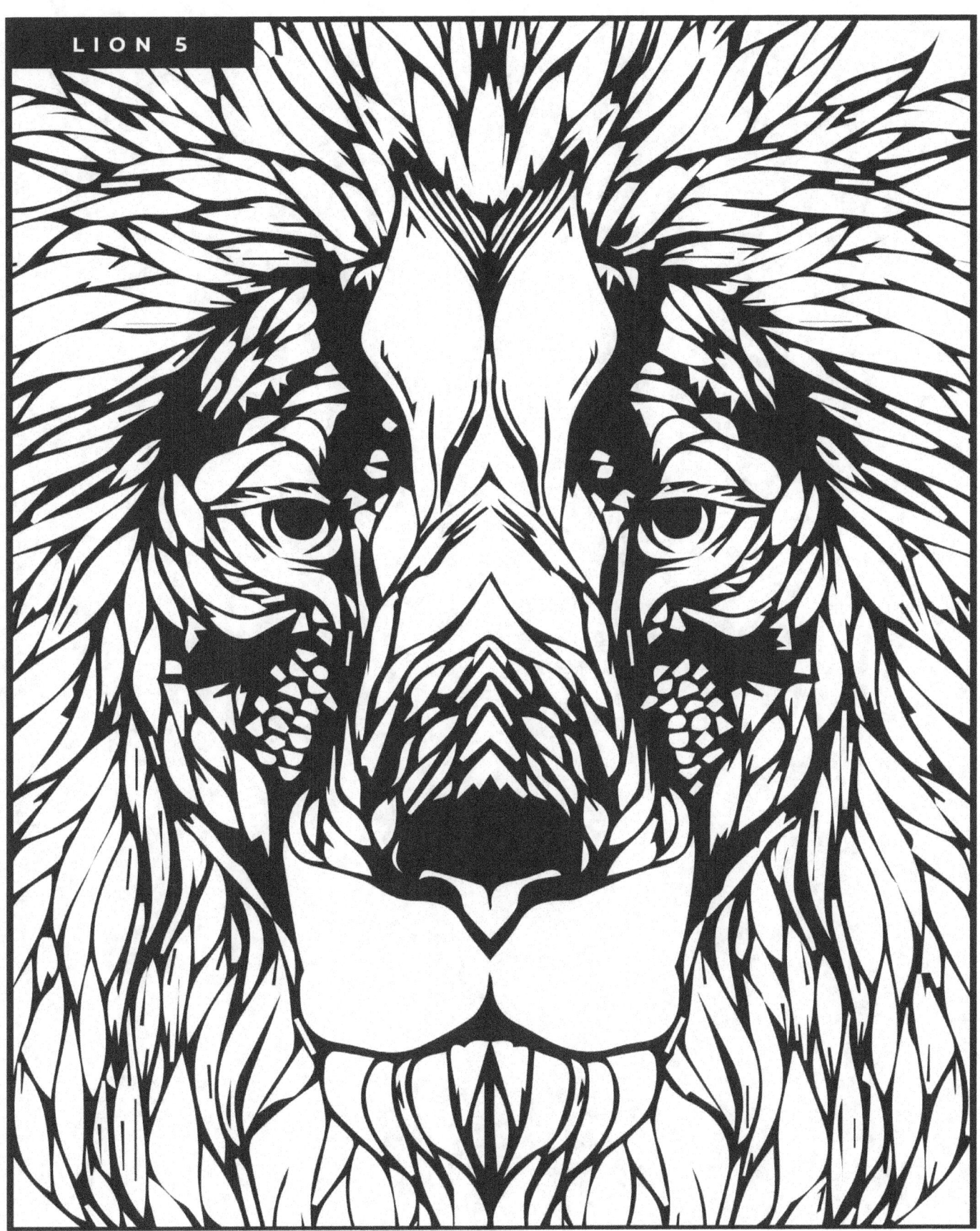

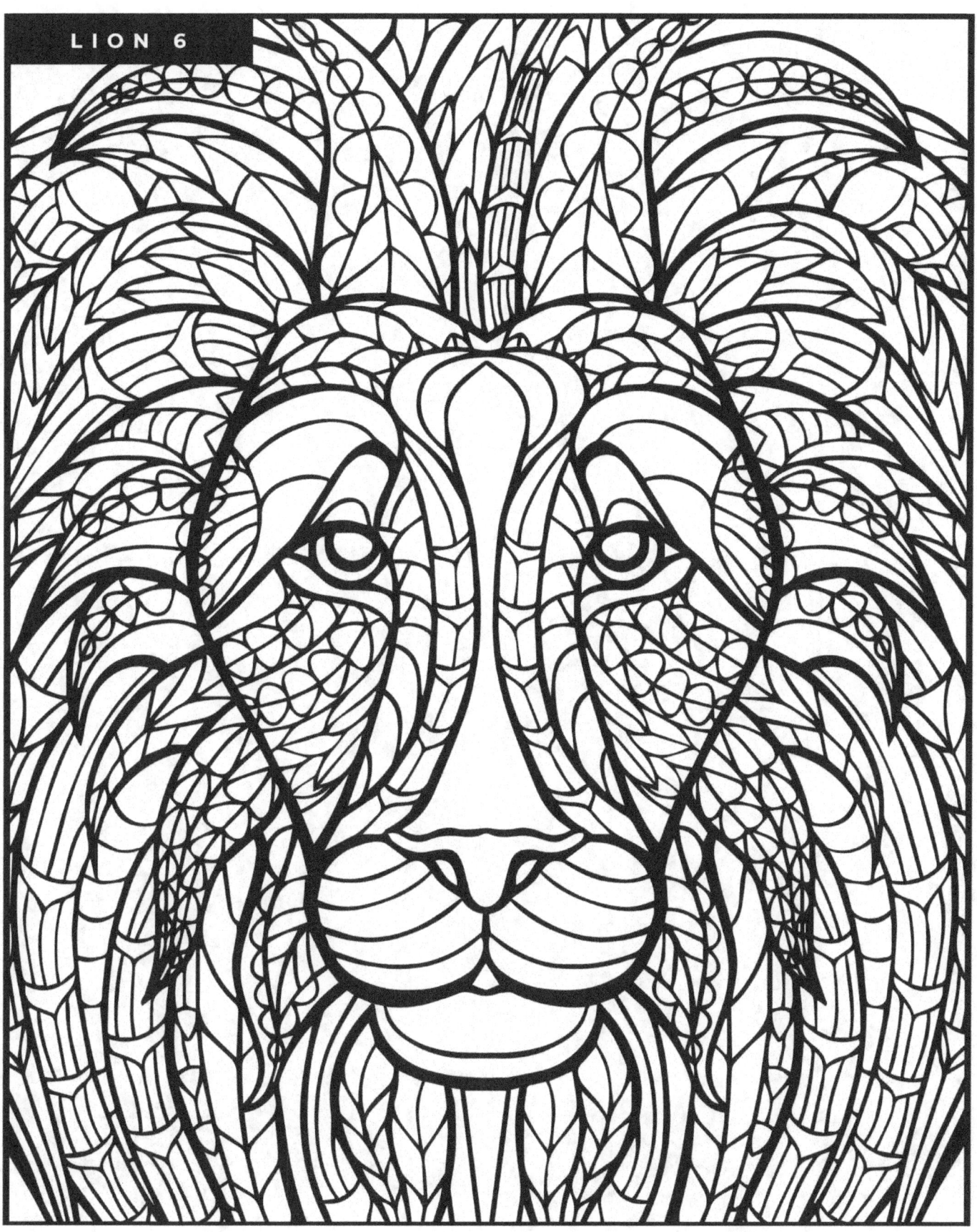

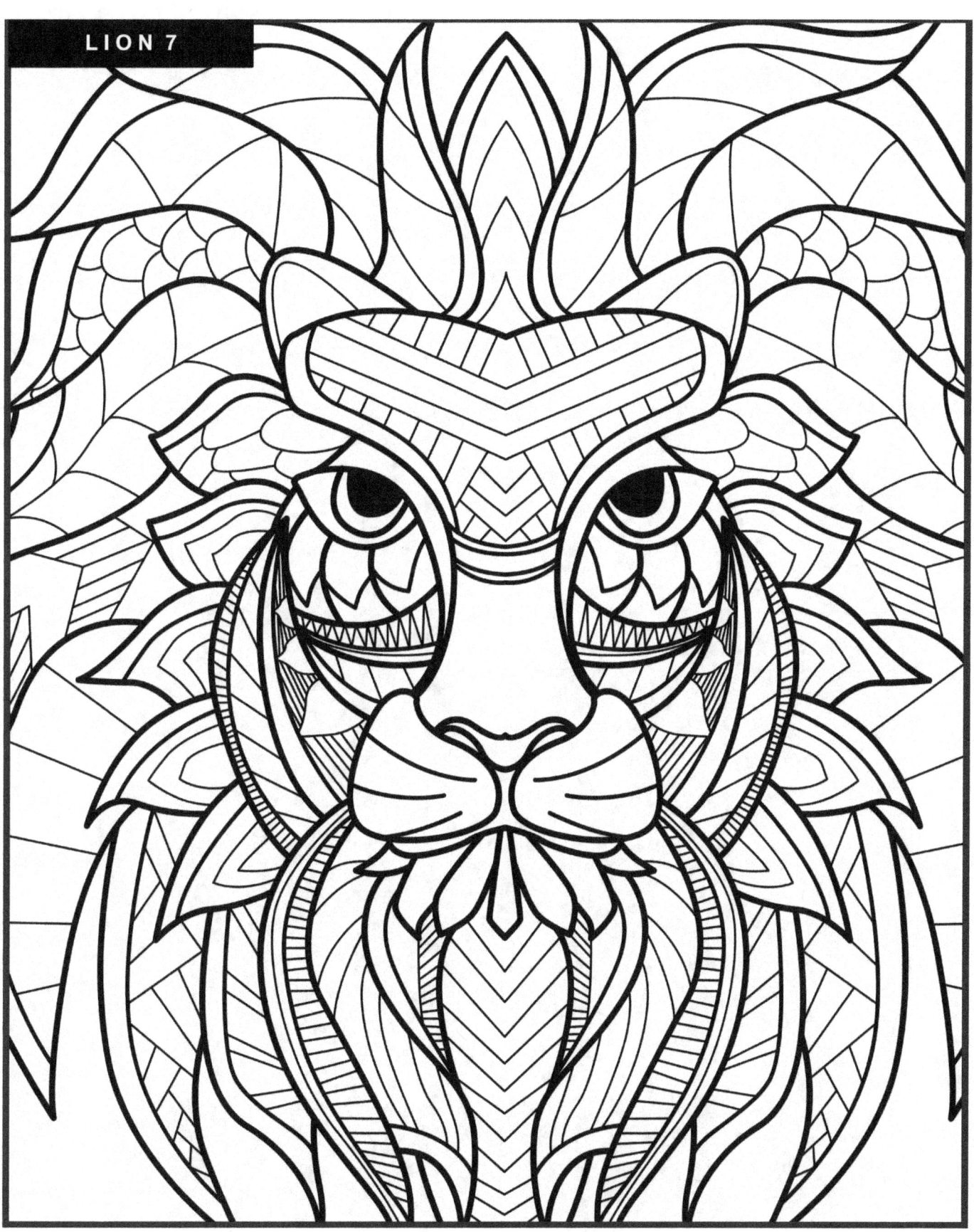

CAT 1

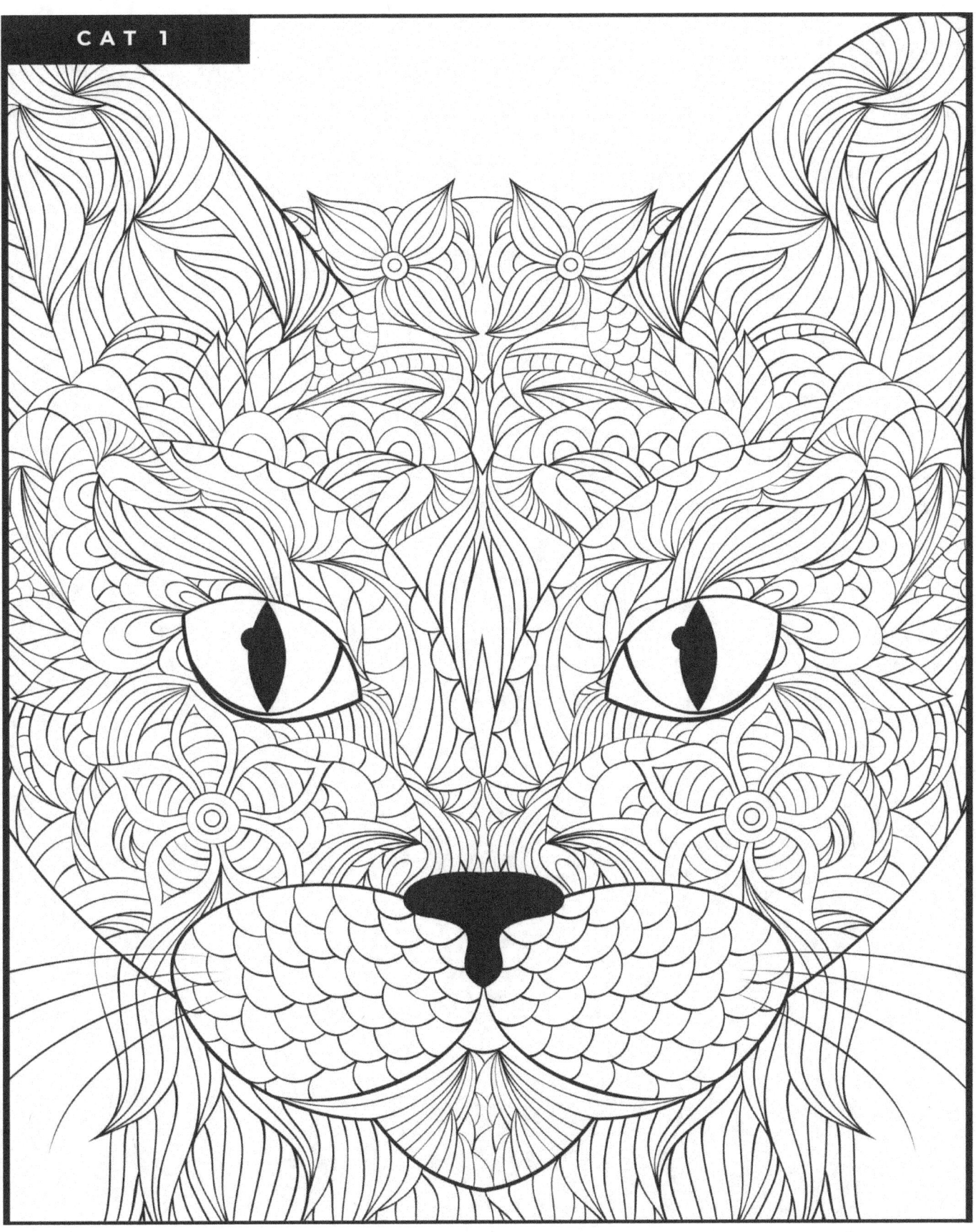

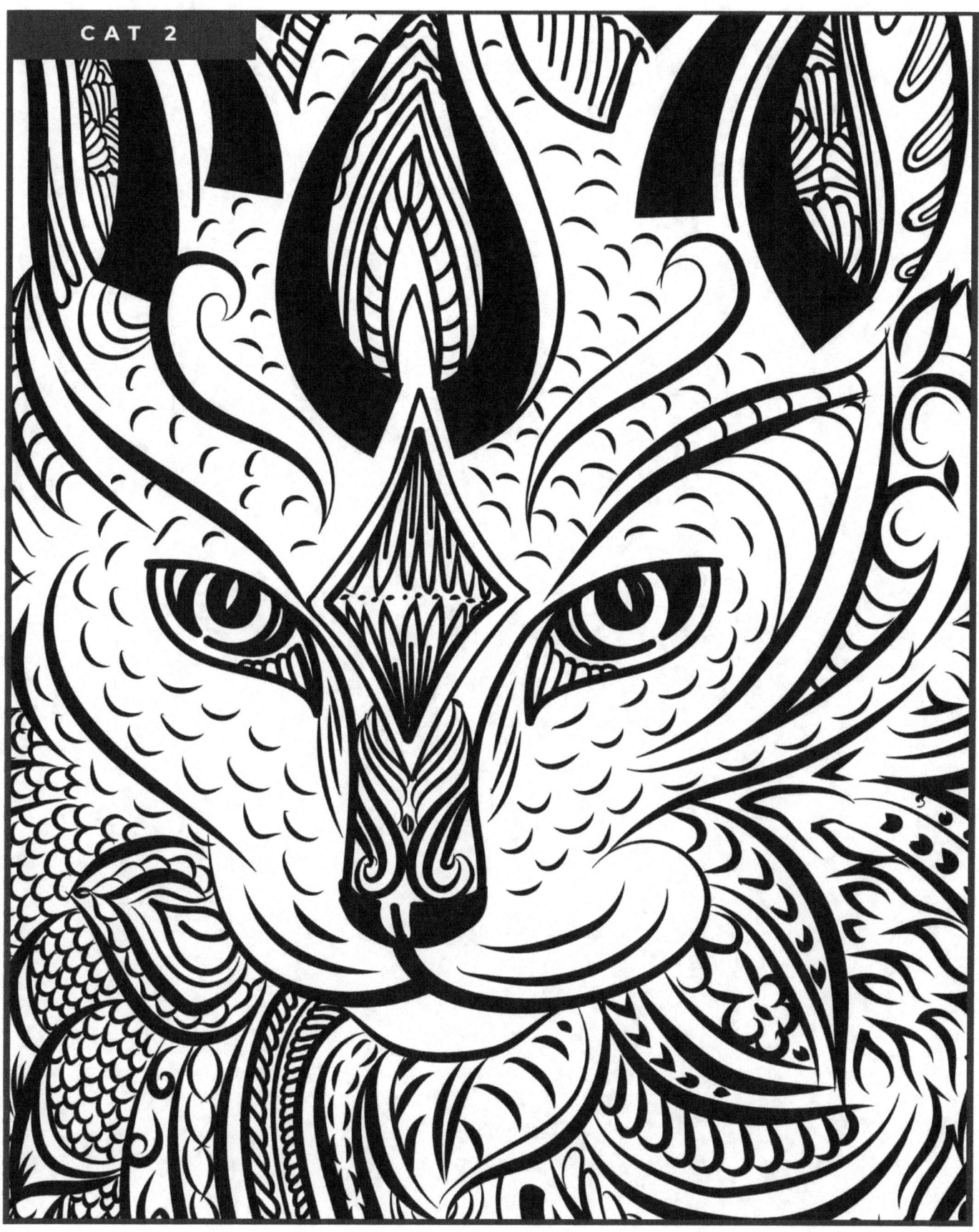

CAT 3

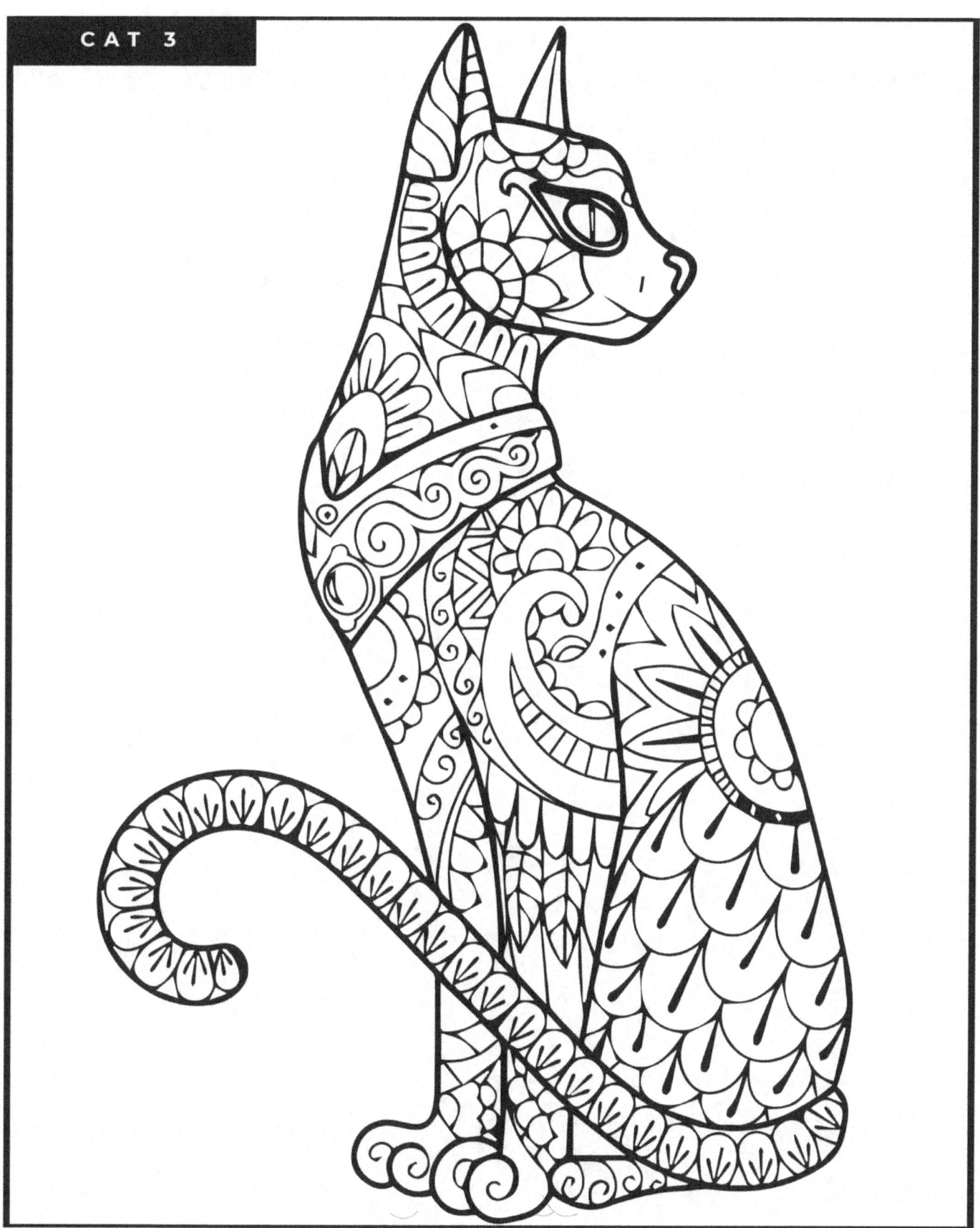

CAT 4

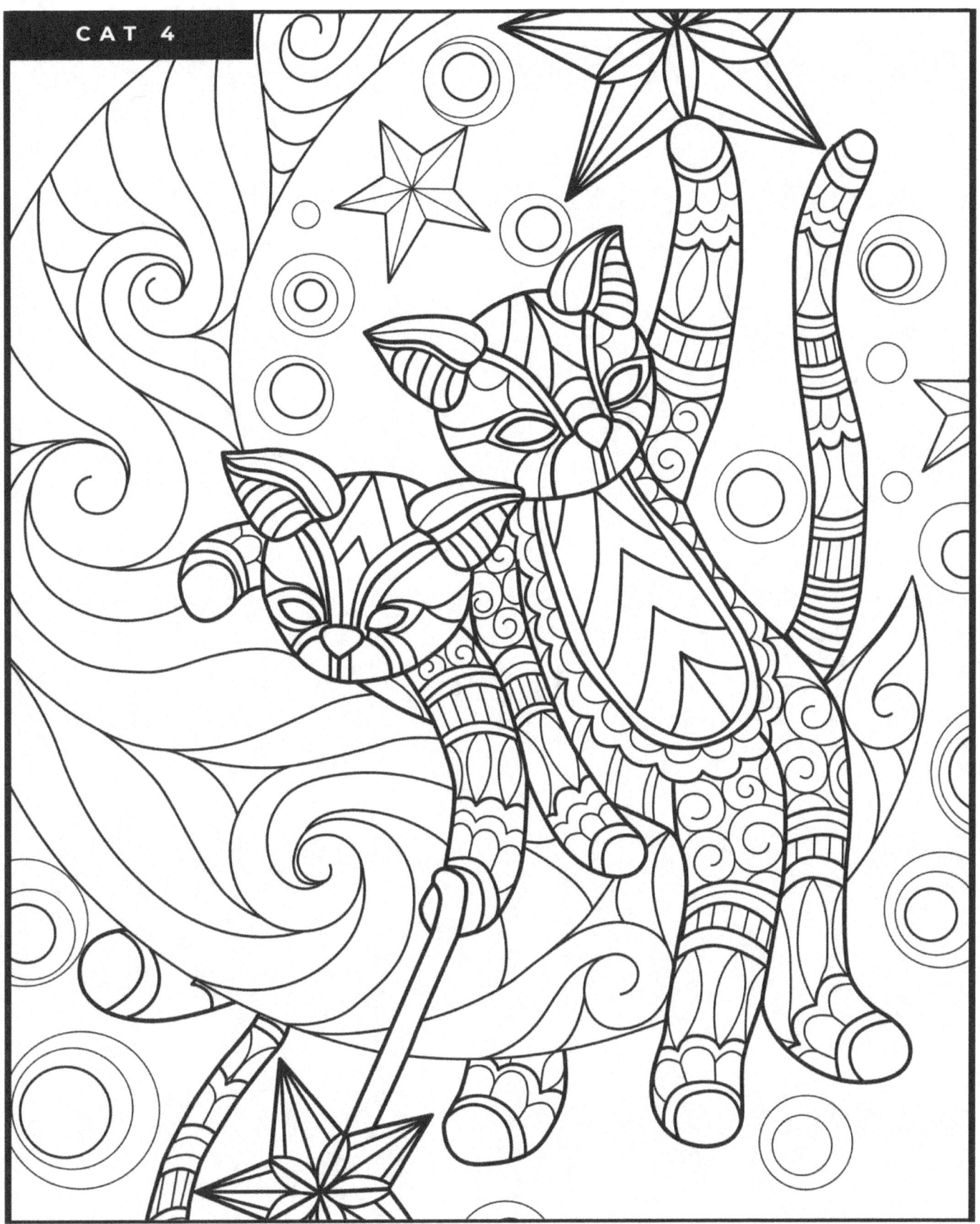

CAT 5

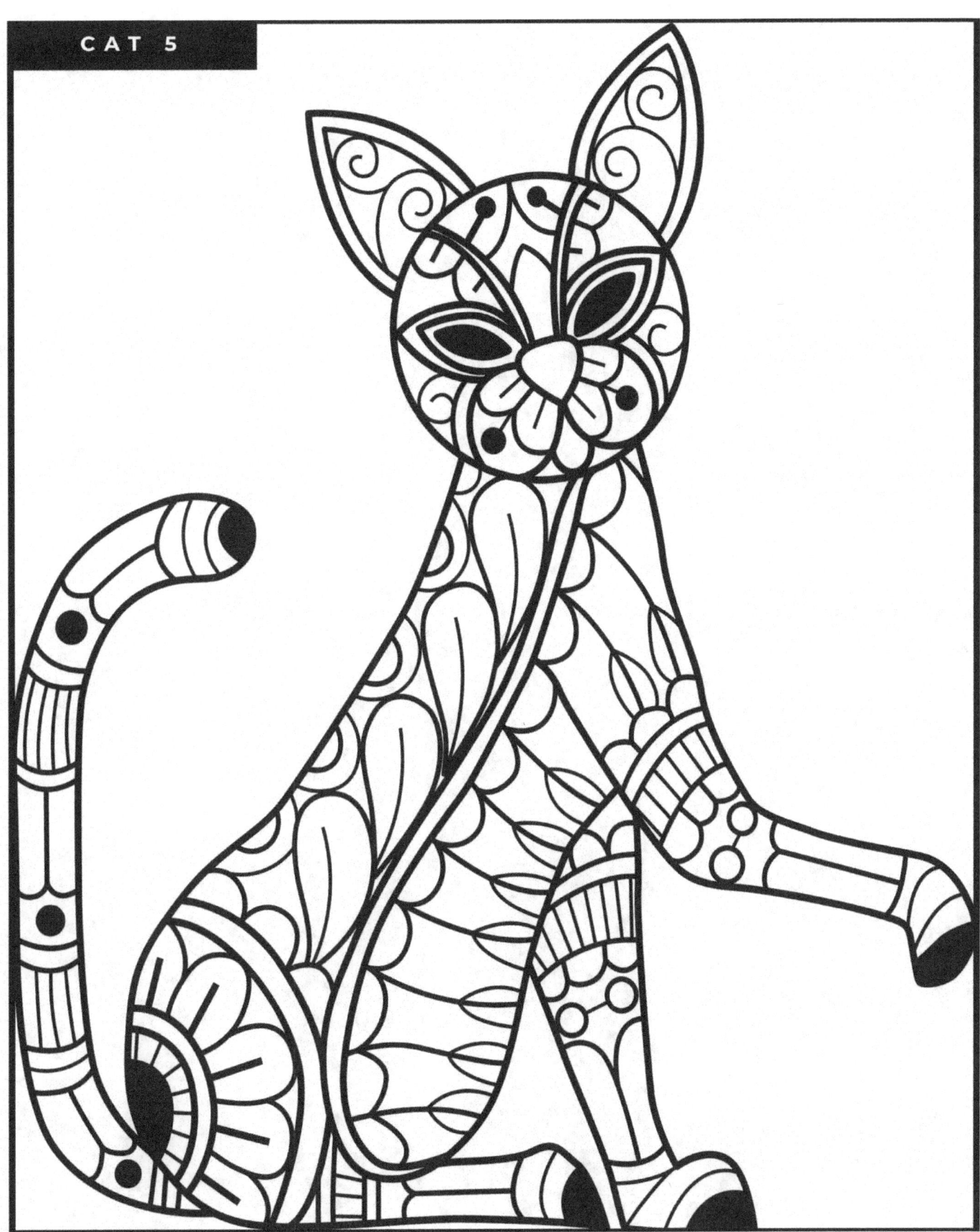

CAT 6

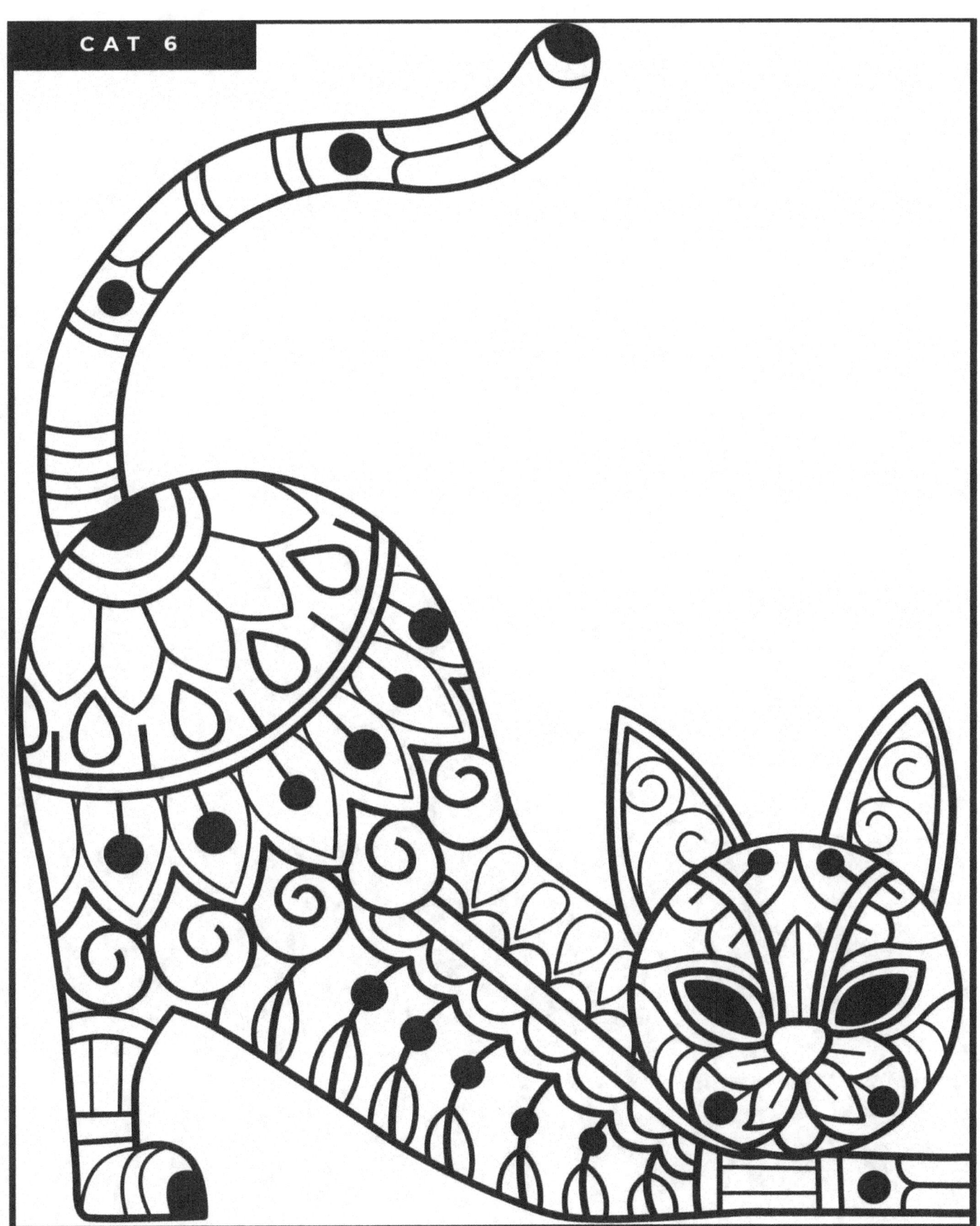

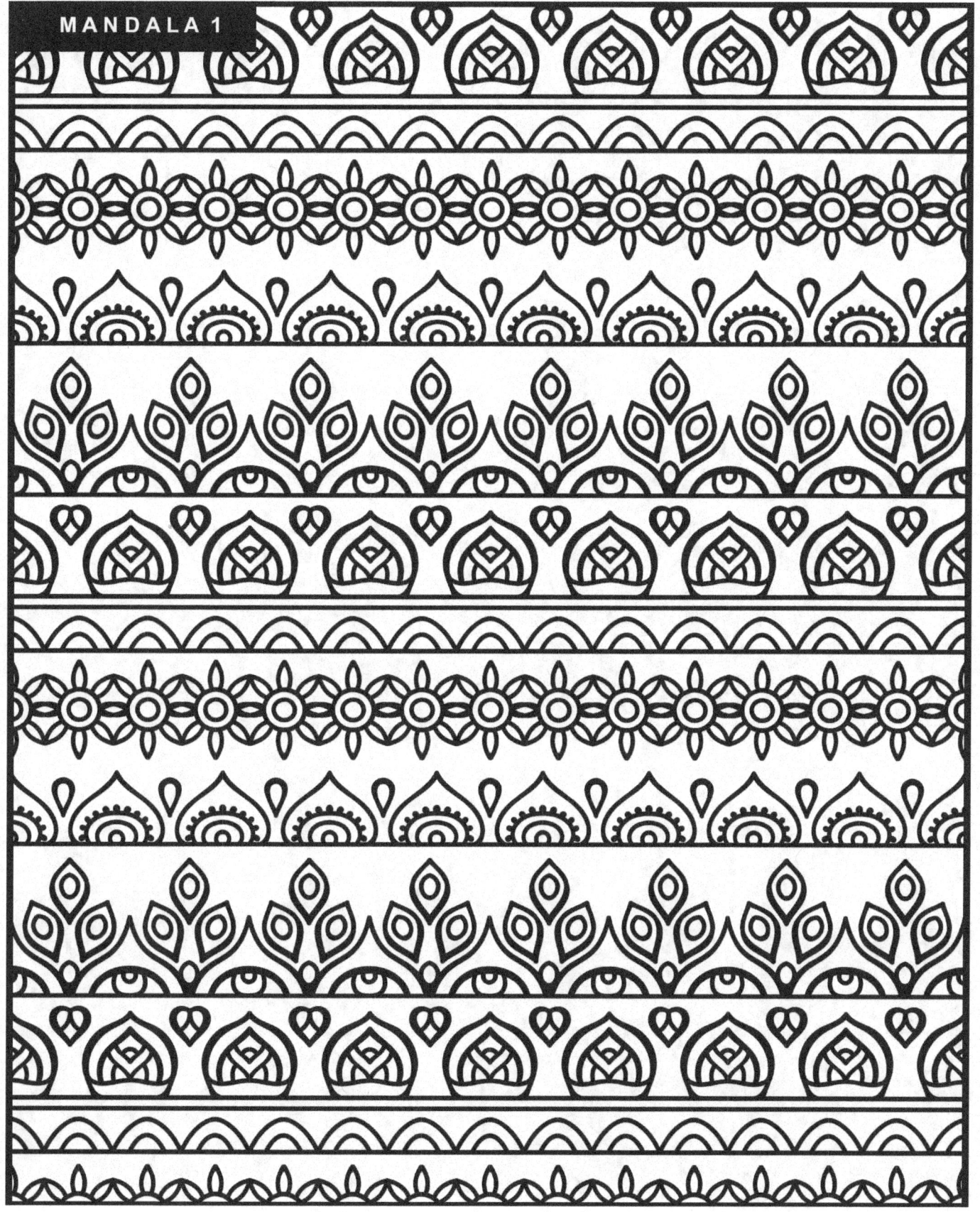

MANDALA 2

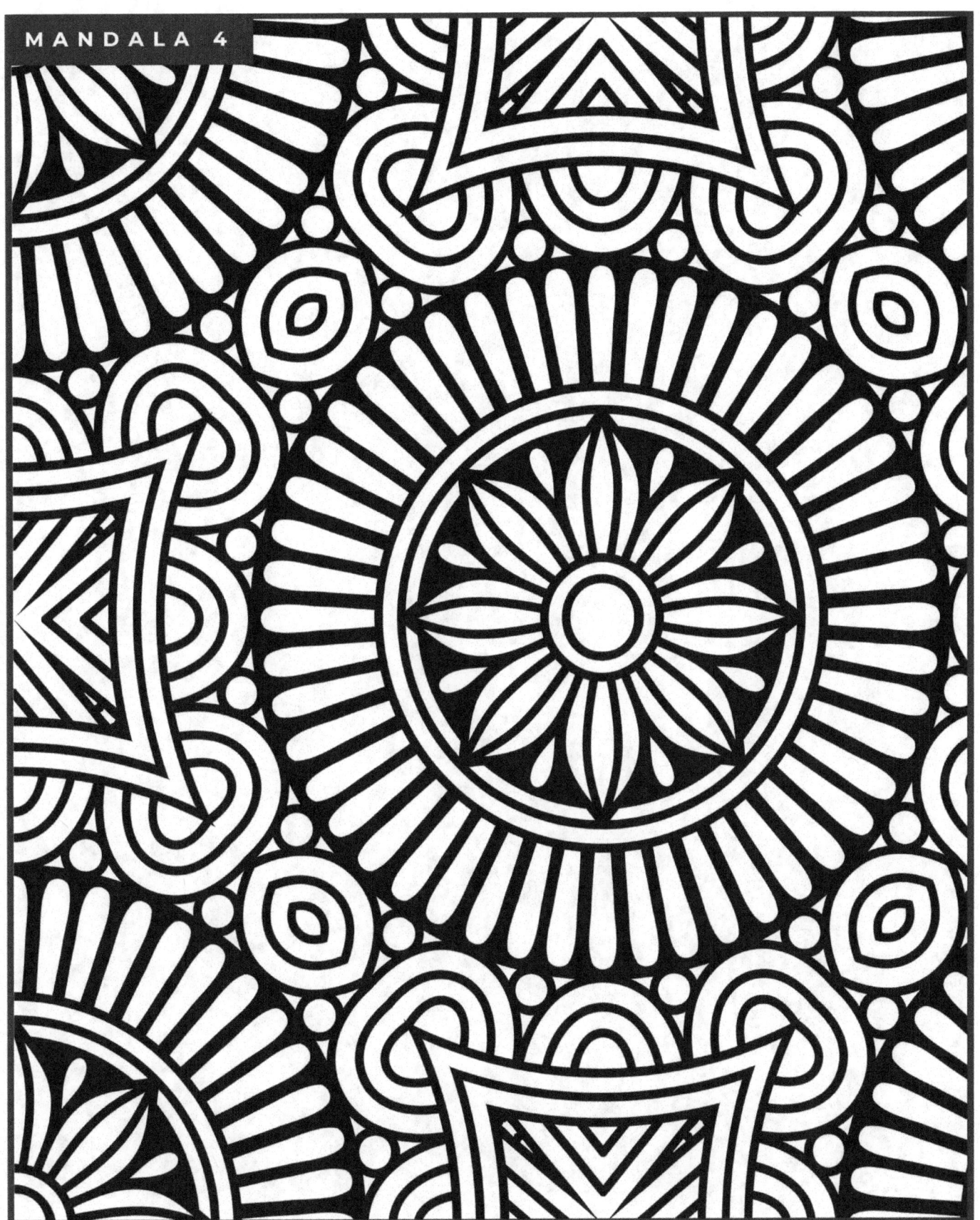

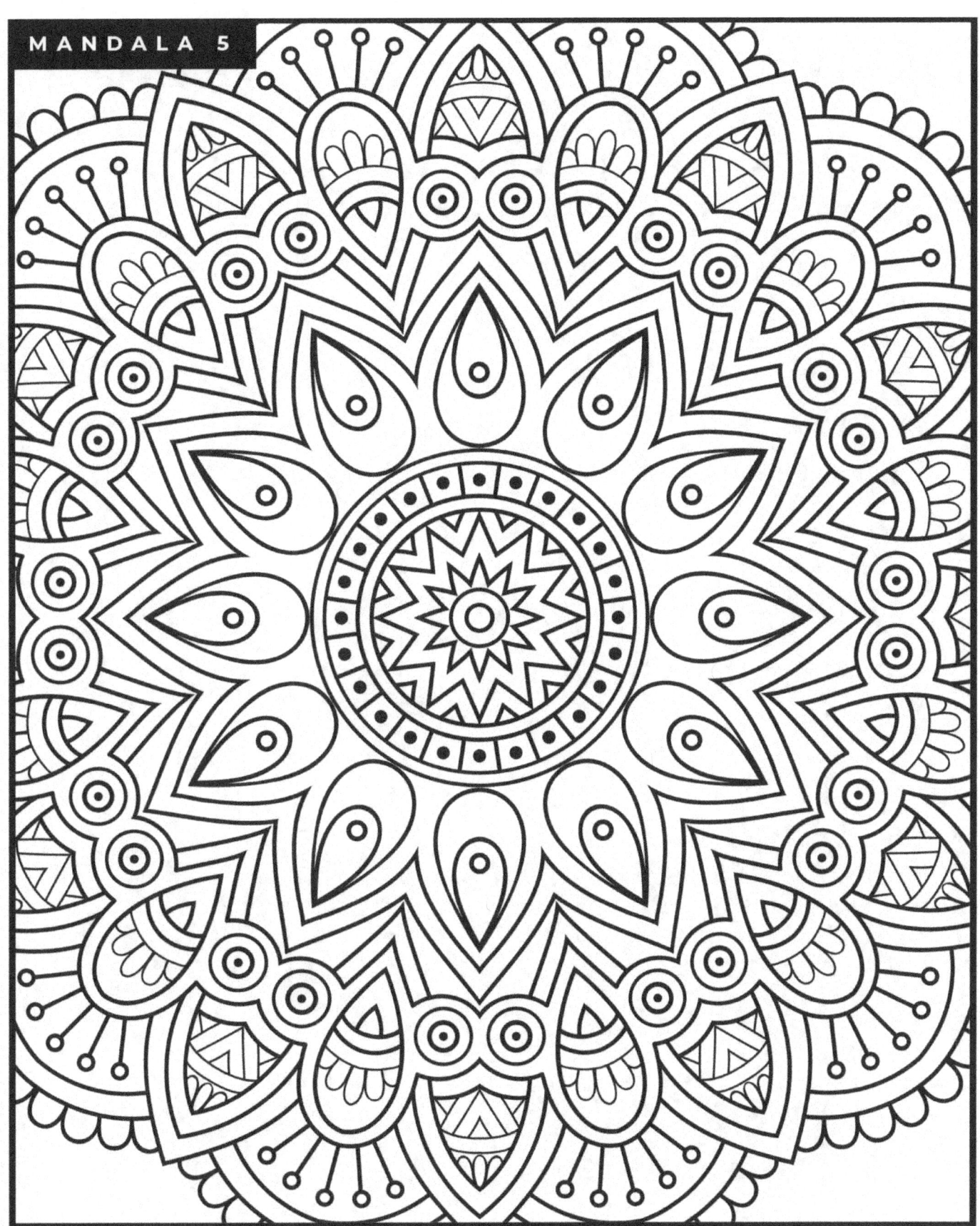

MANDALA 6

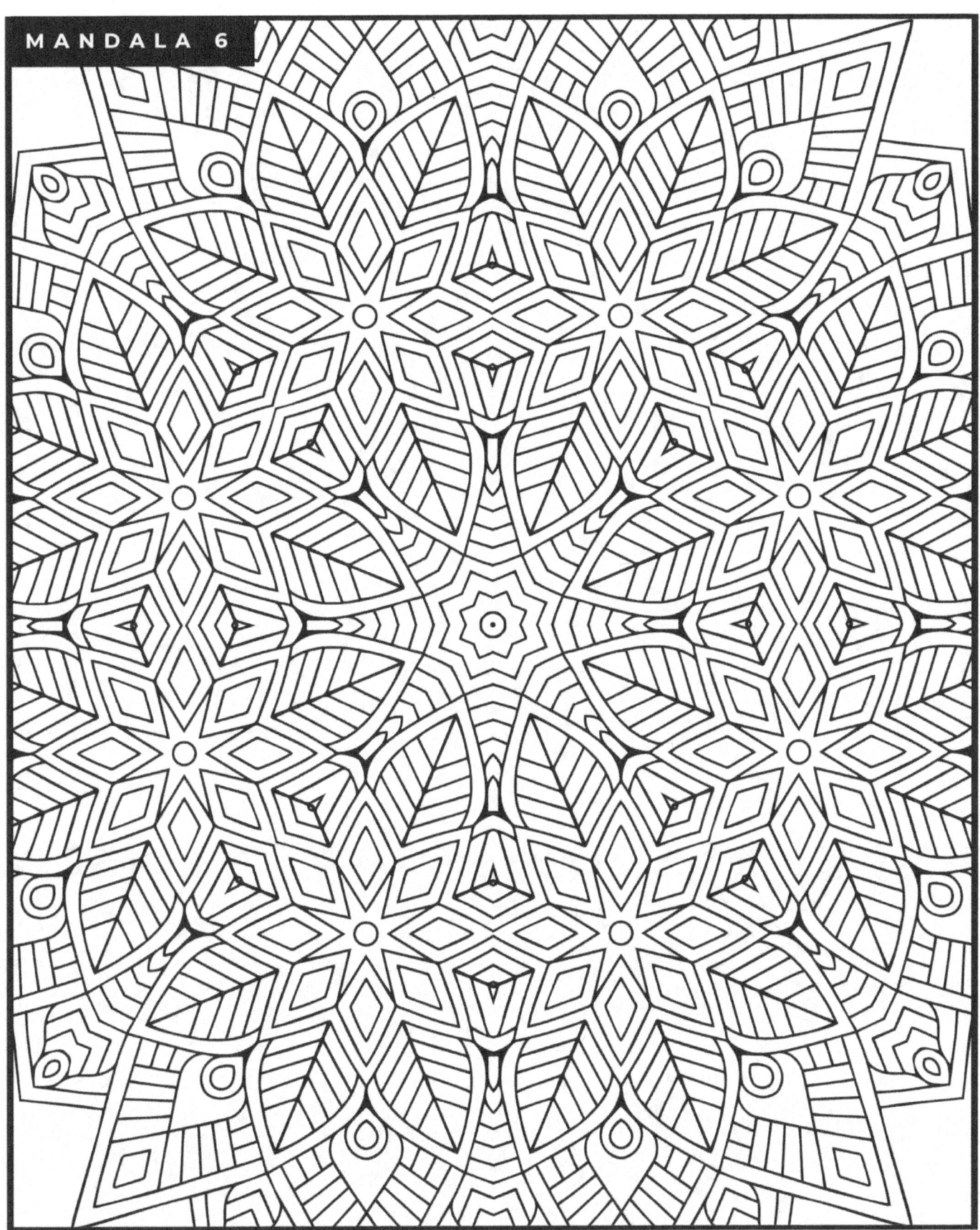

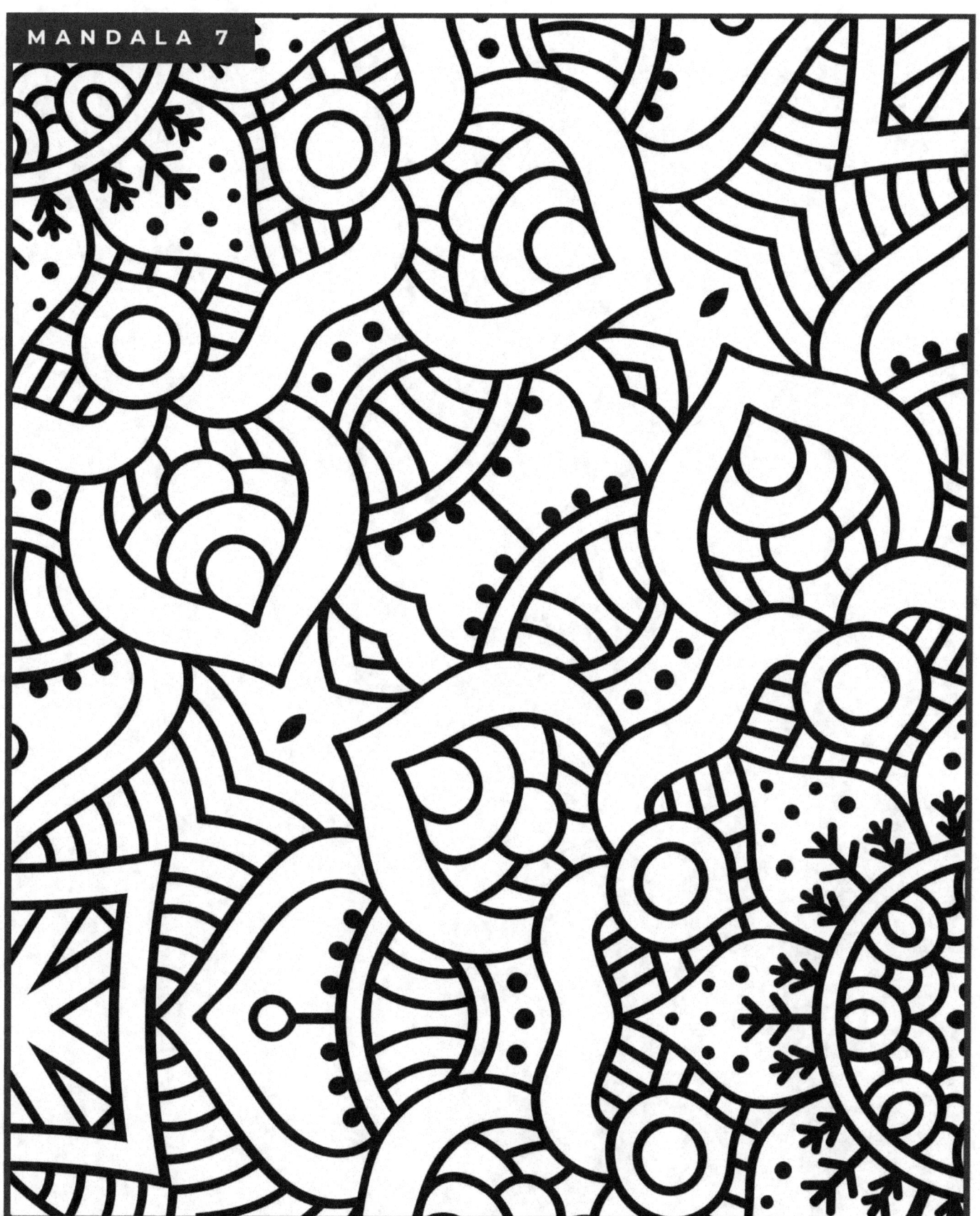

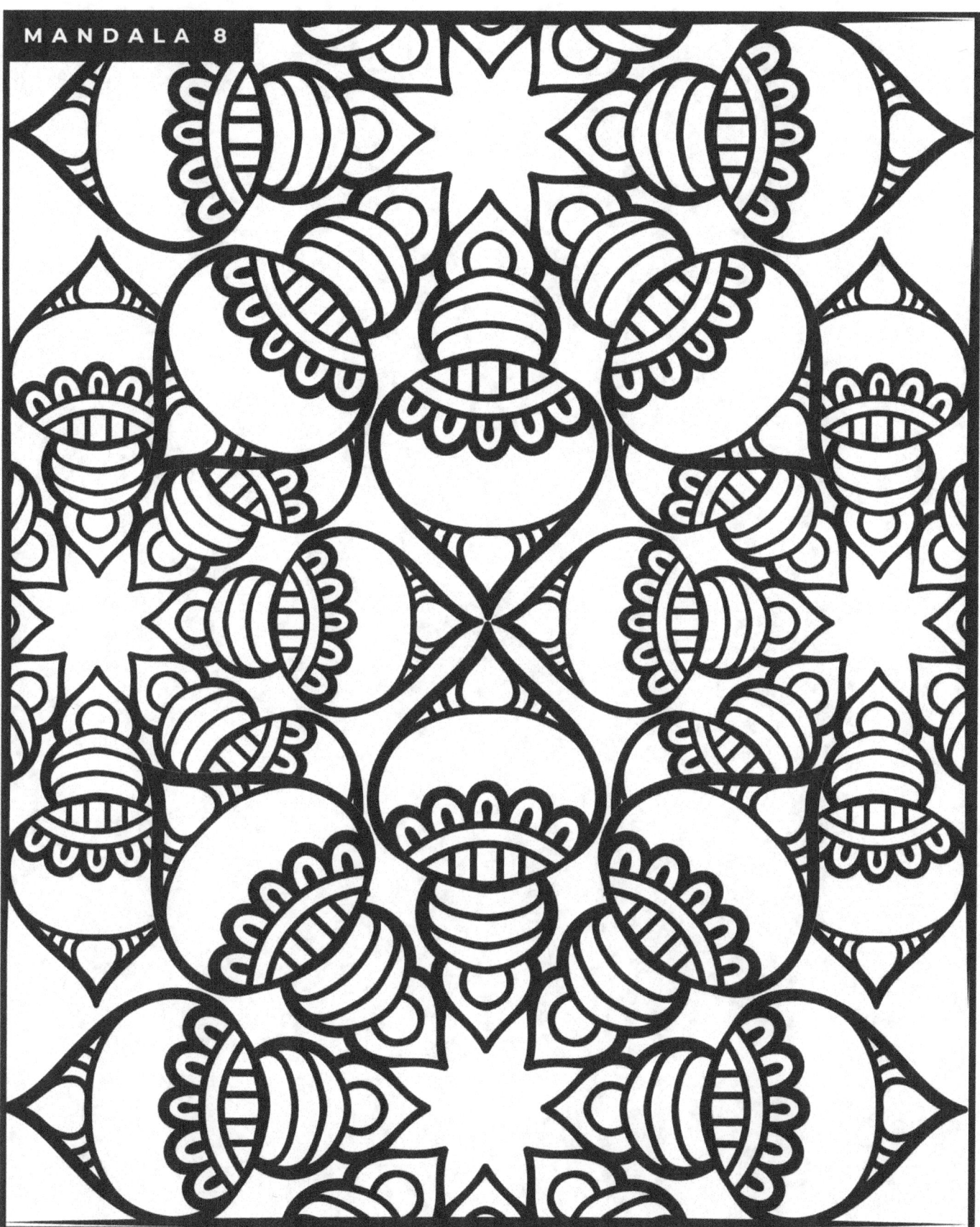

MANDALA 9

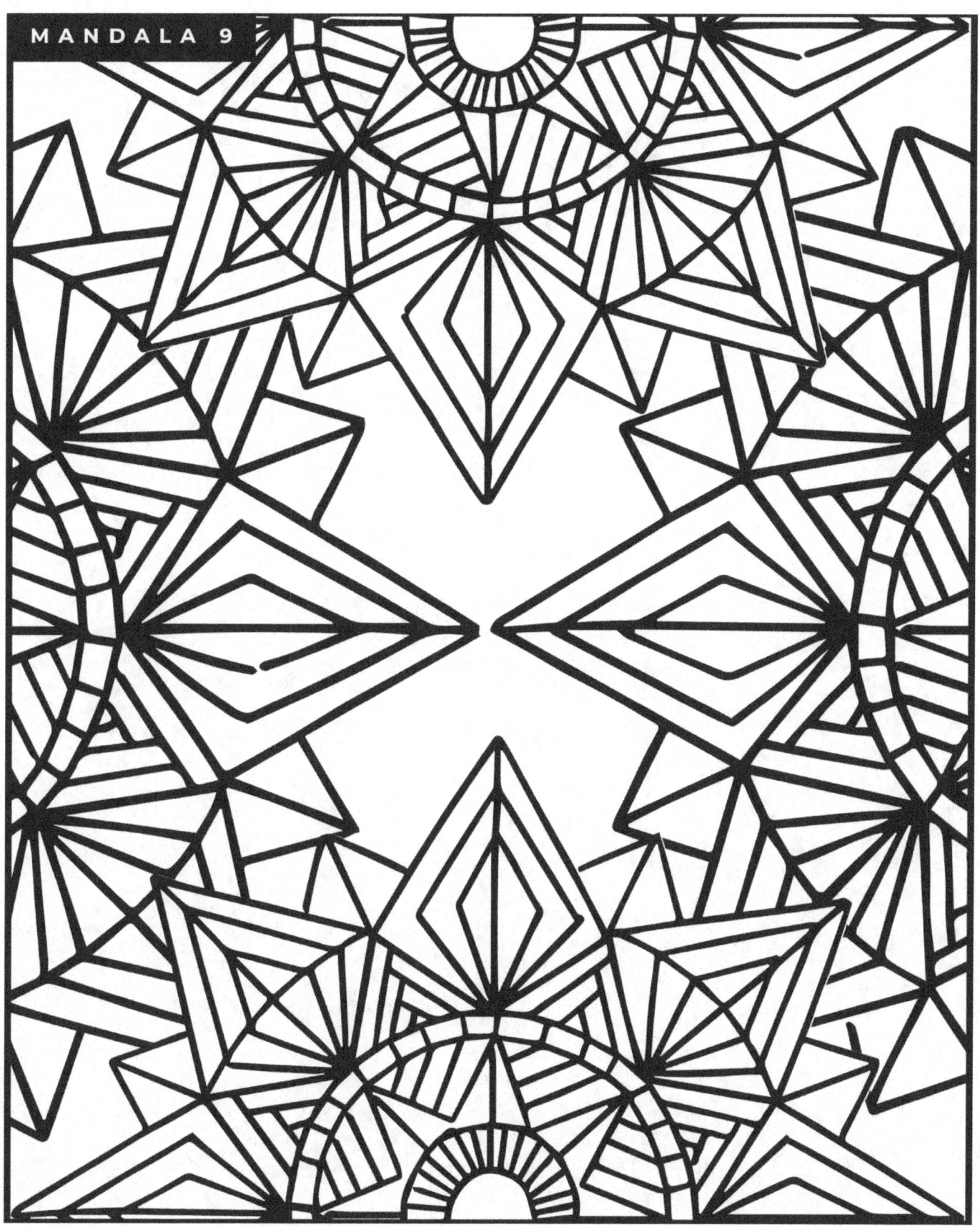

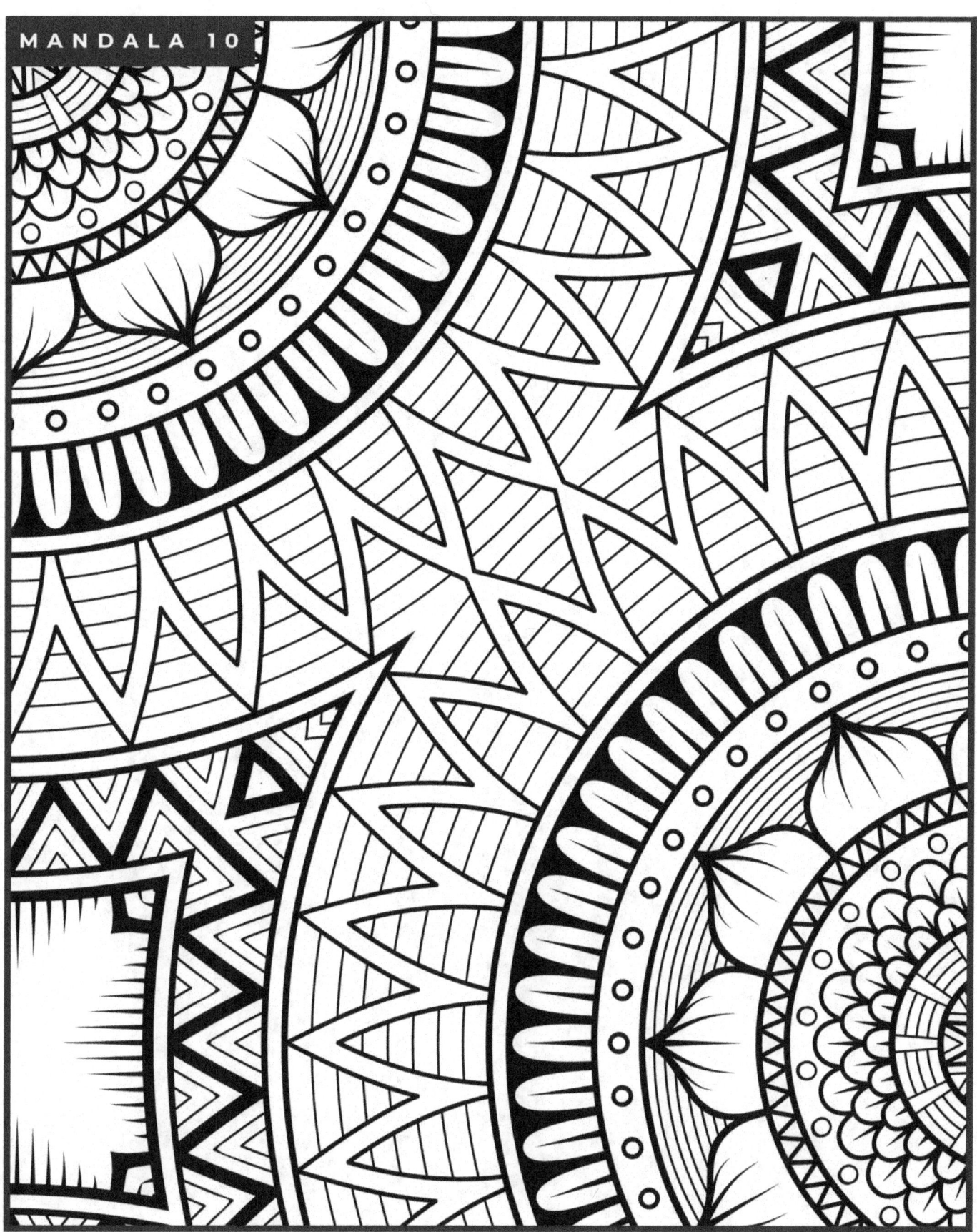

MANDALA 12

DOG 1

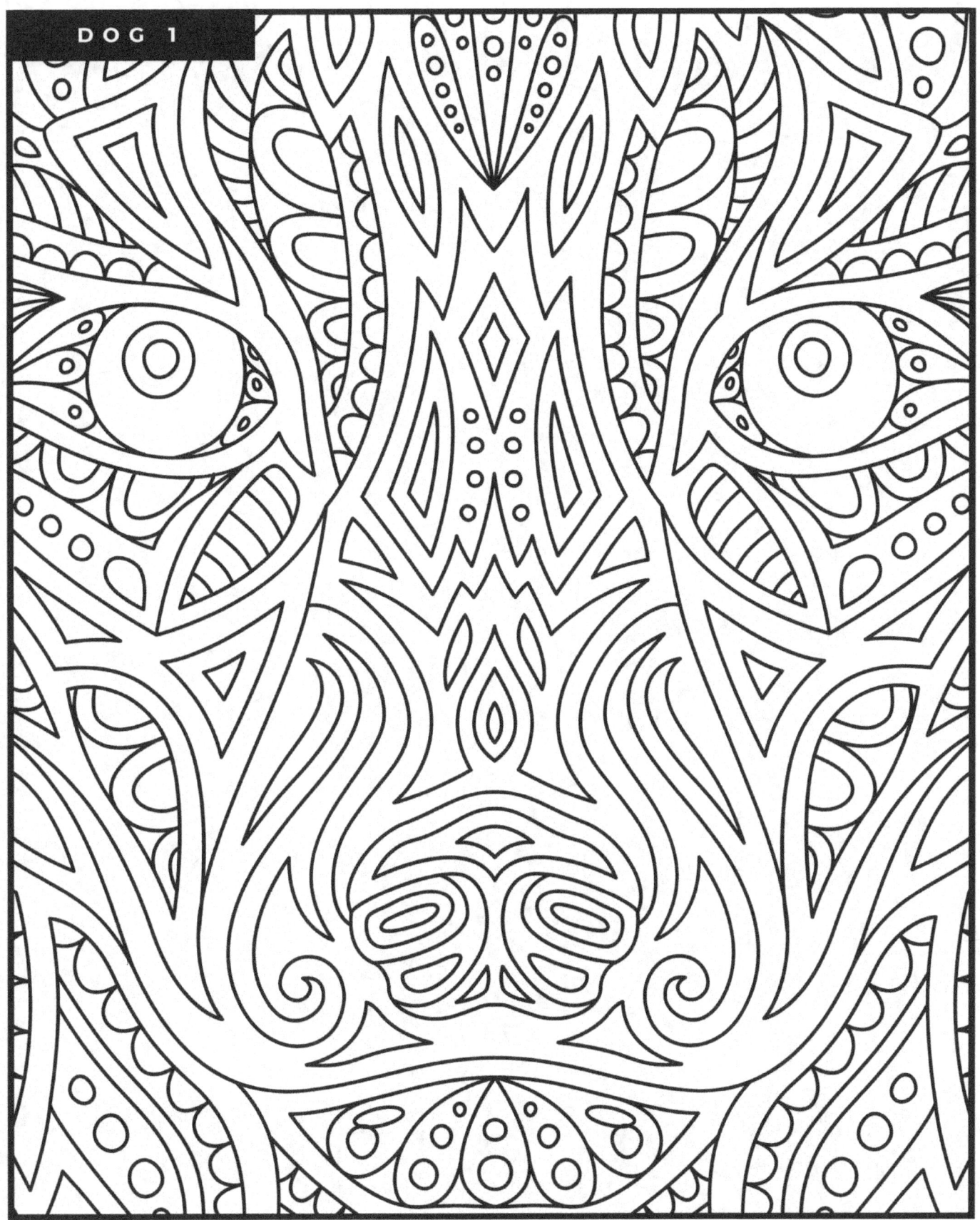

DOG 2

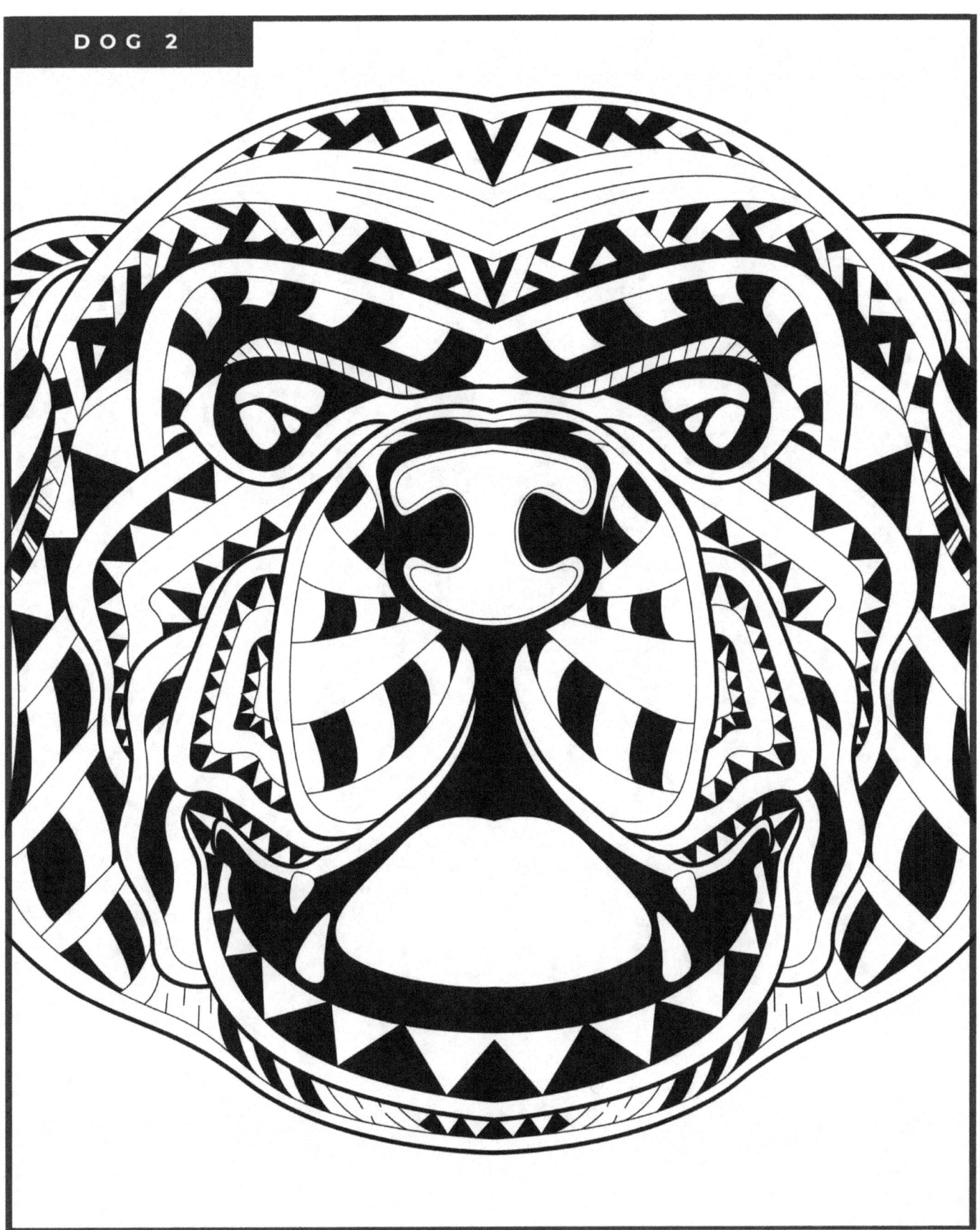

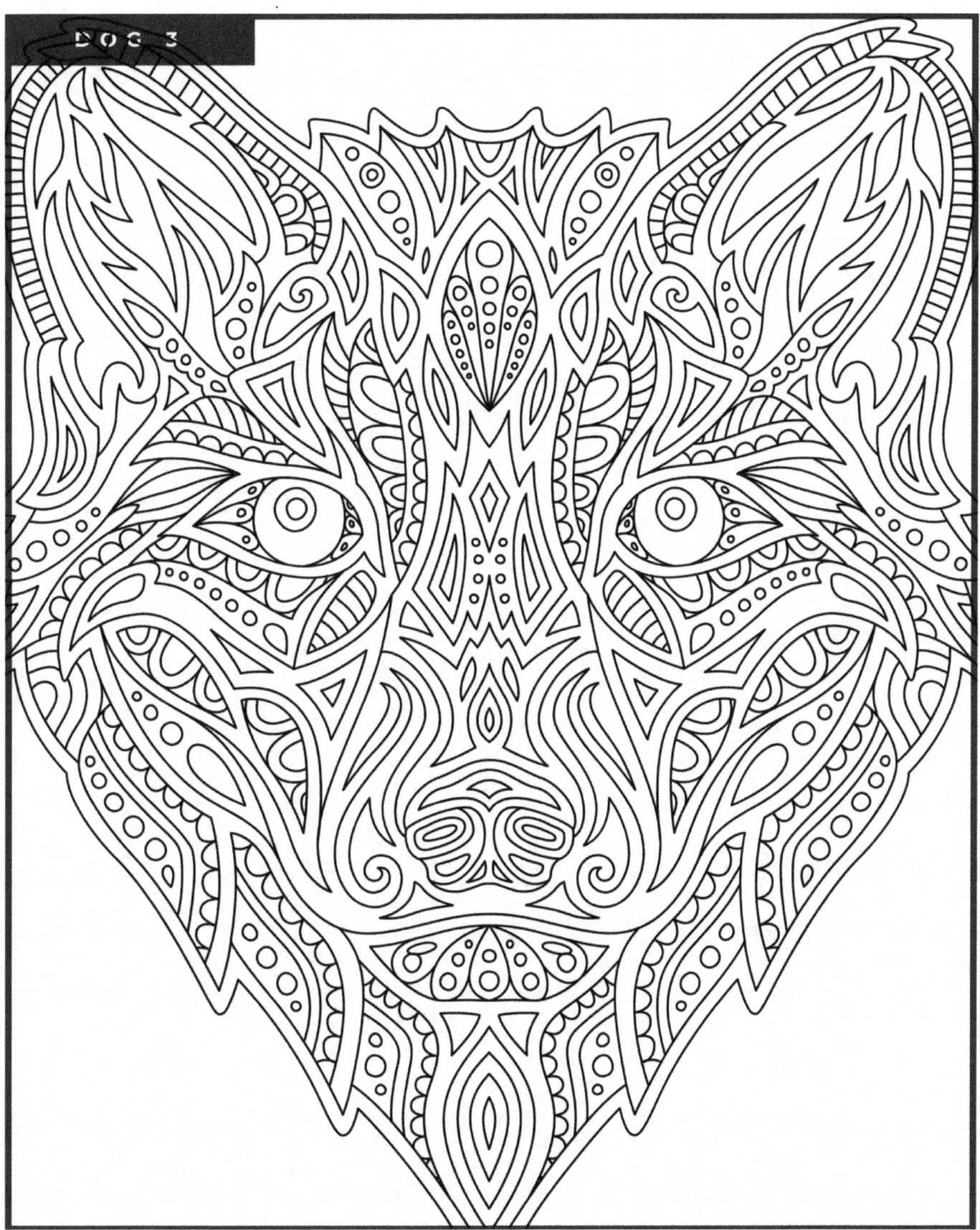

DOG 4

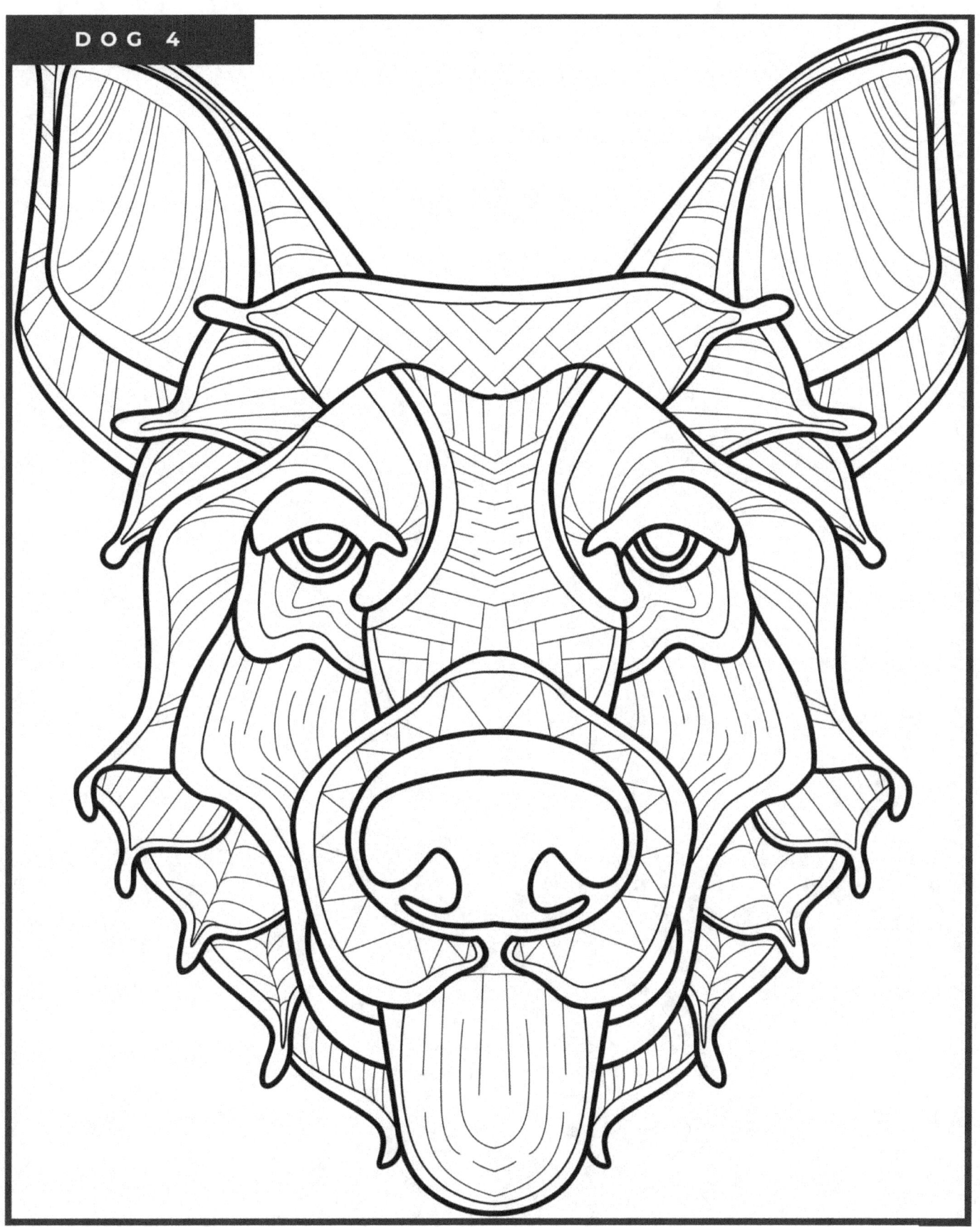

DOG 5

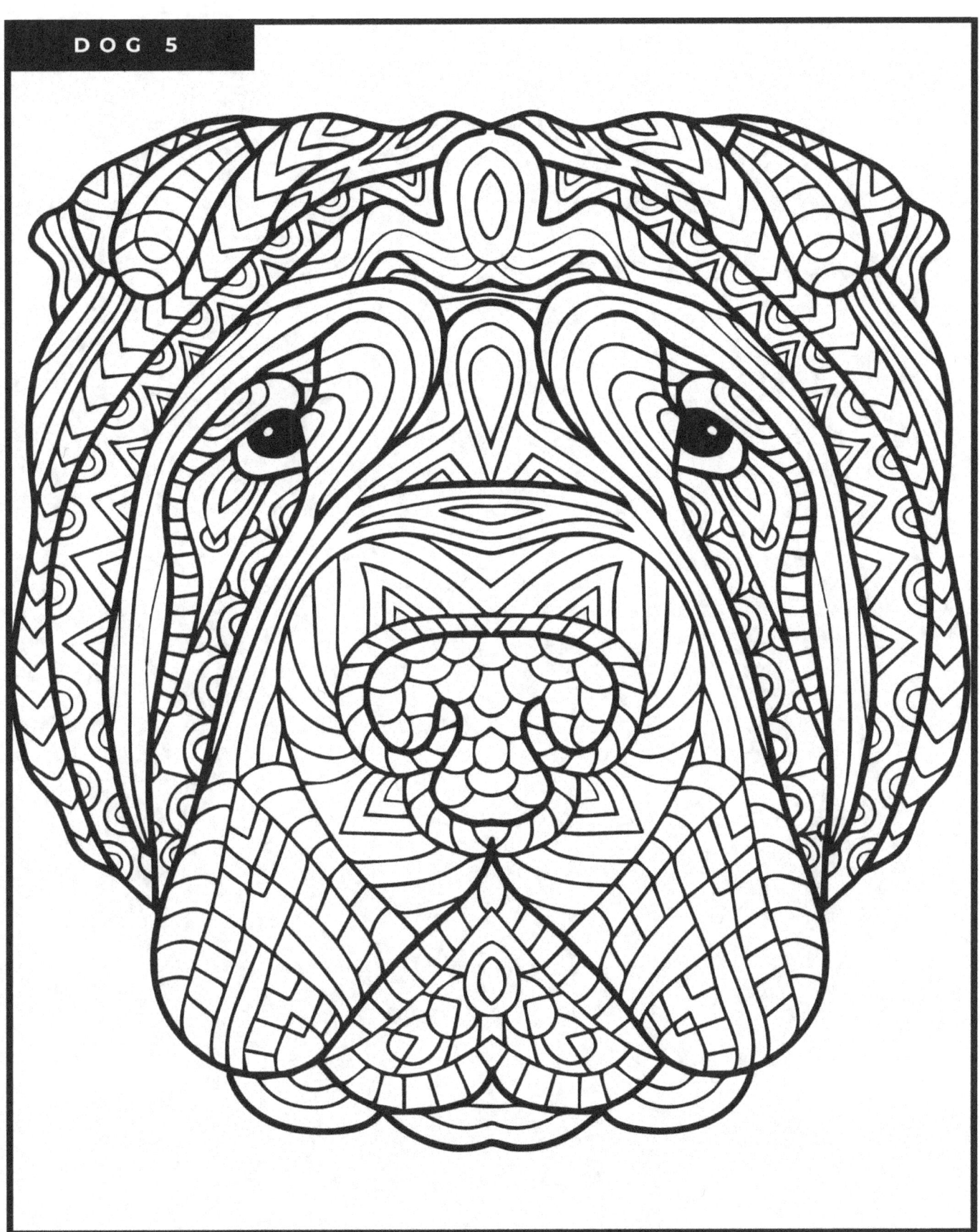

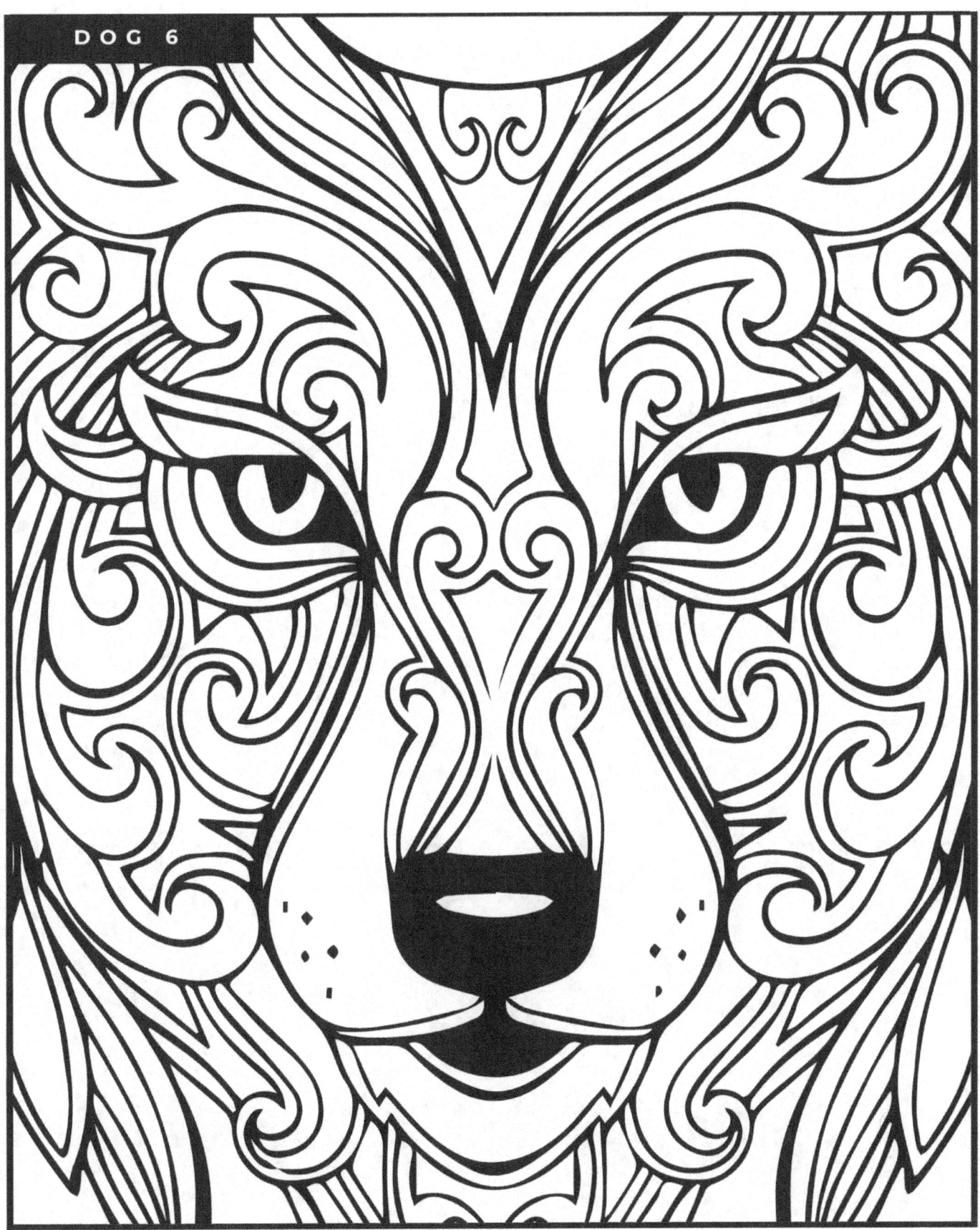

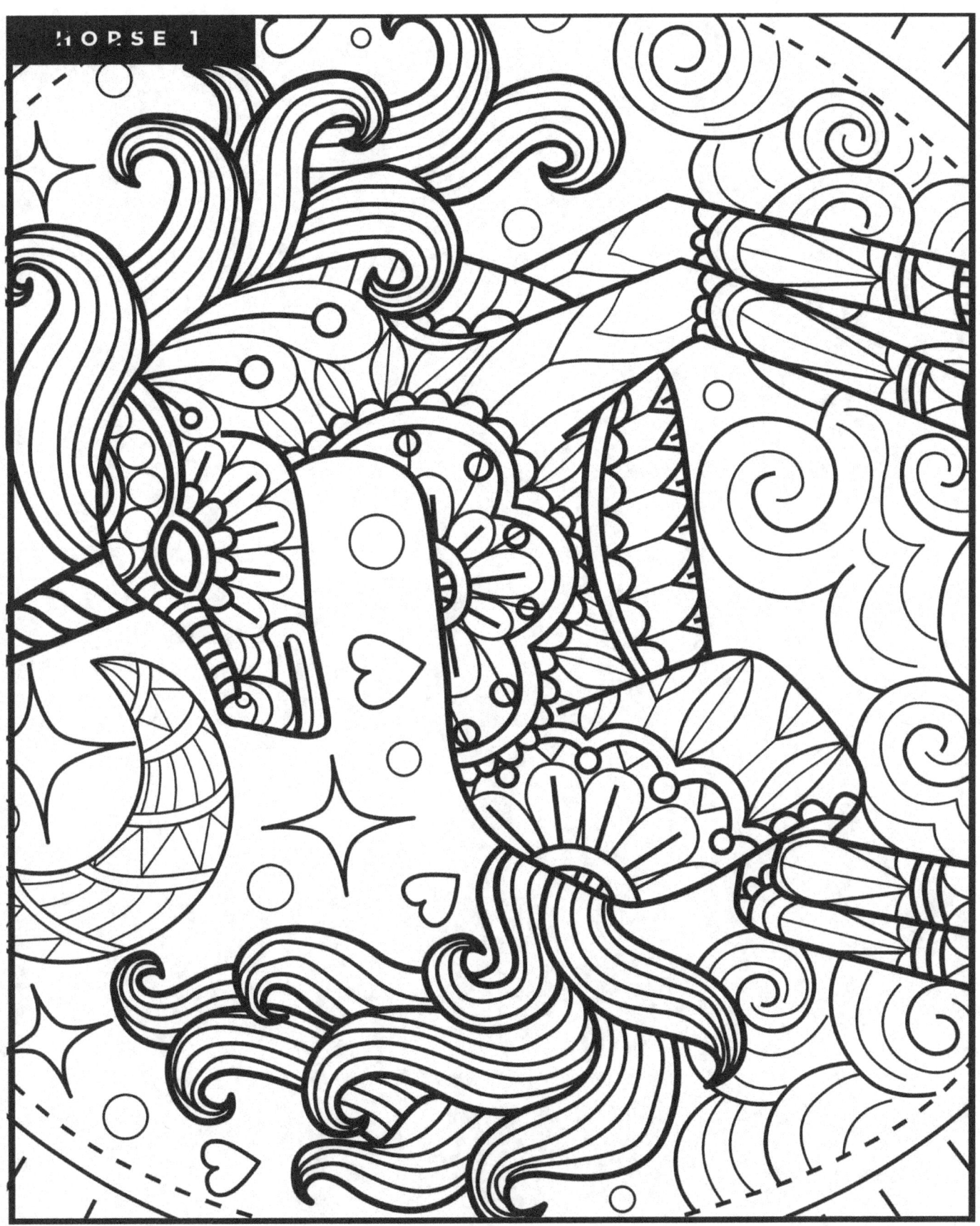

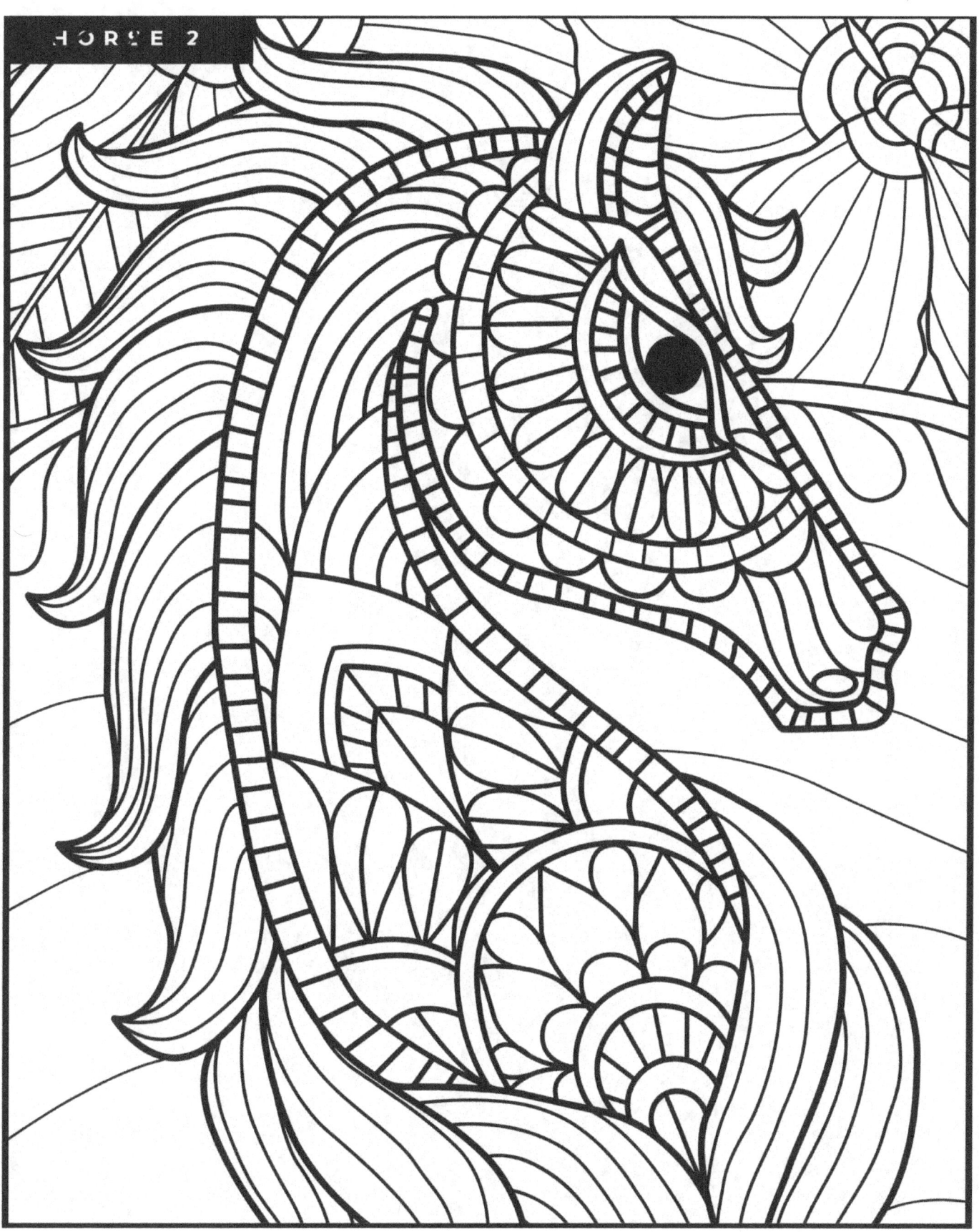

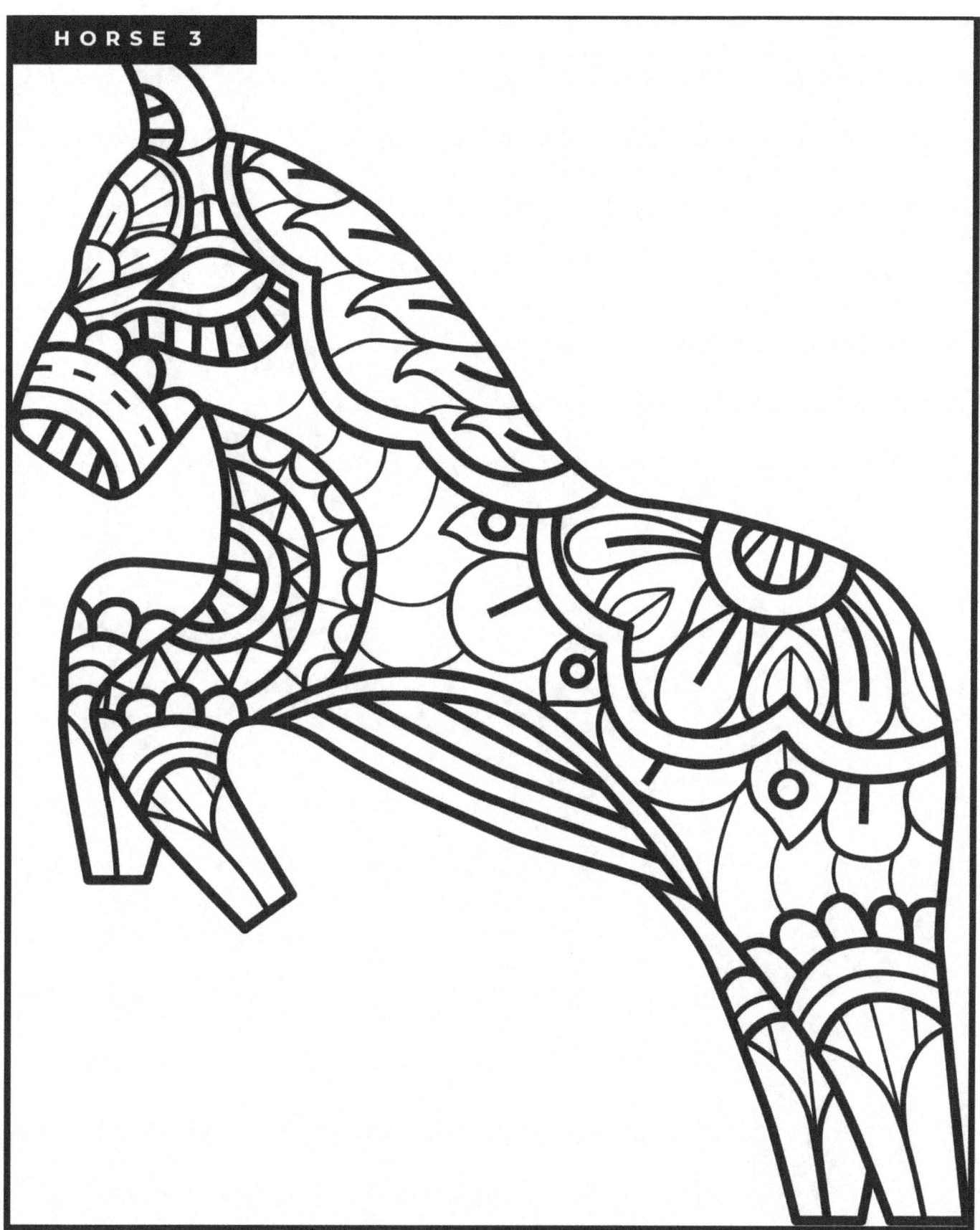

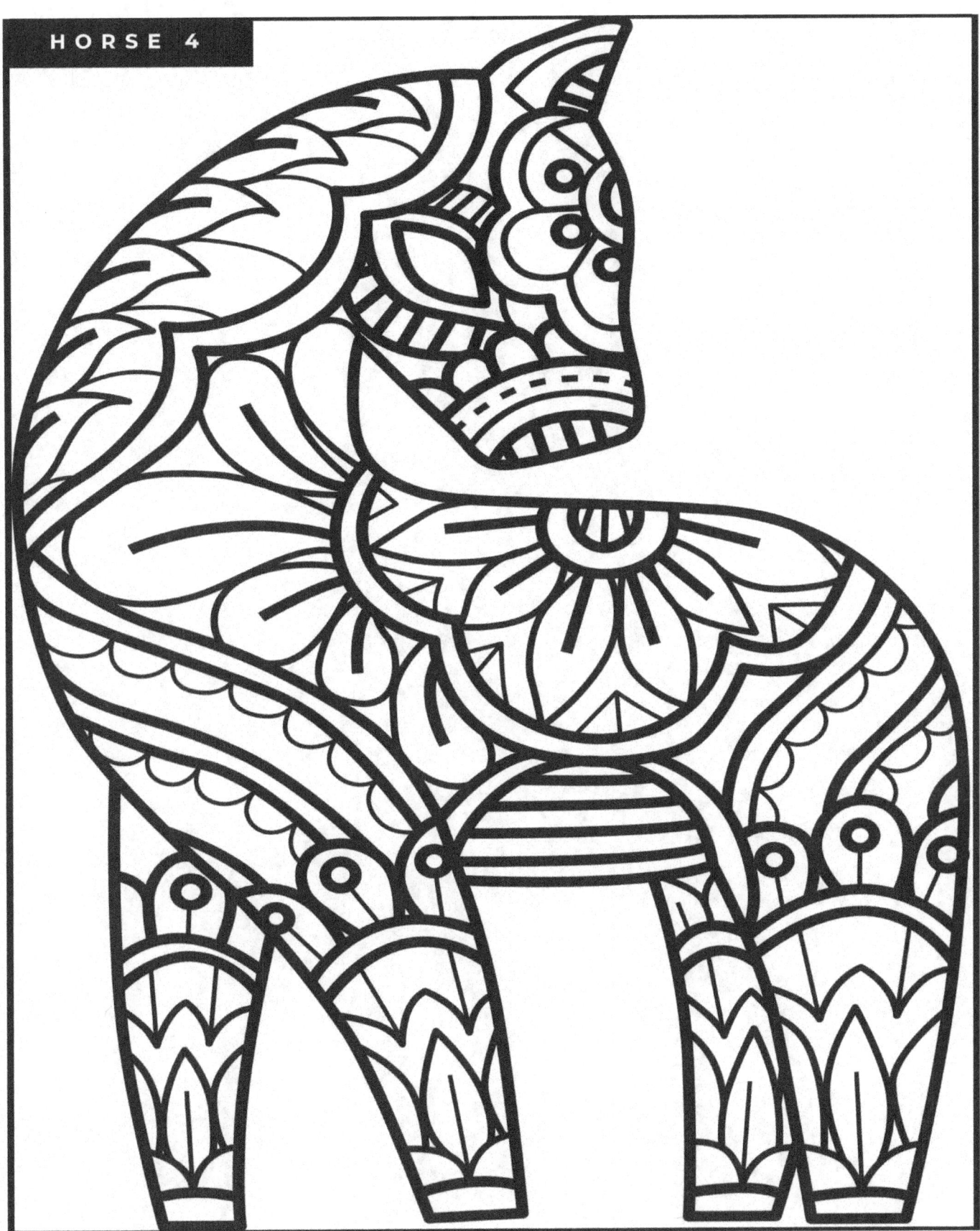

HORSE 5

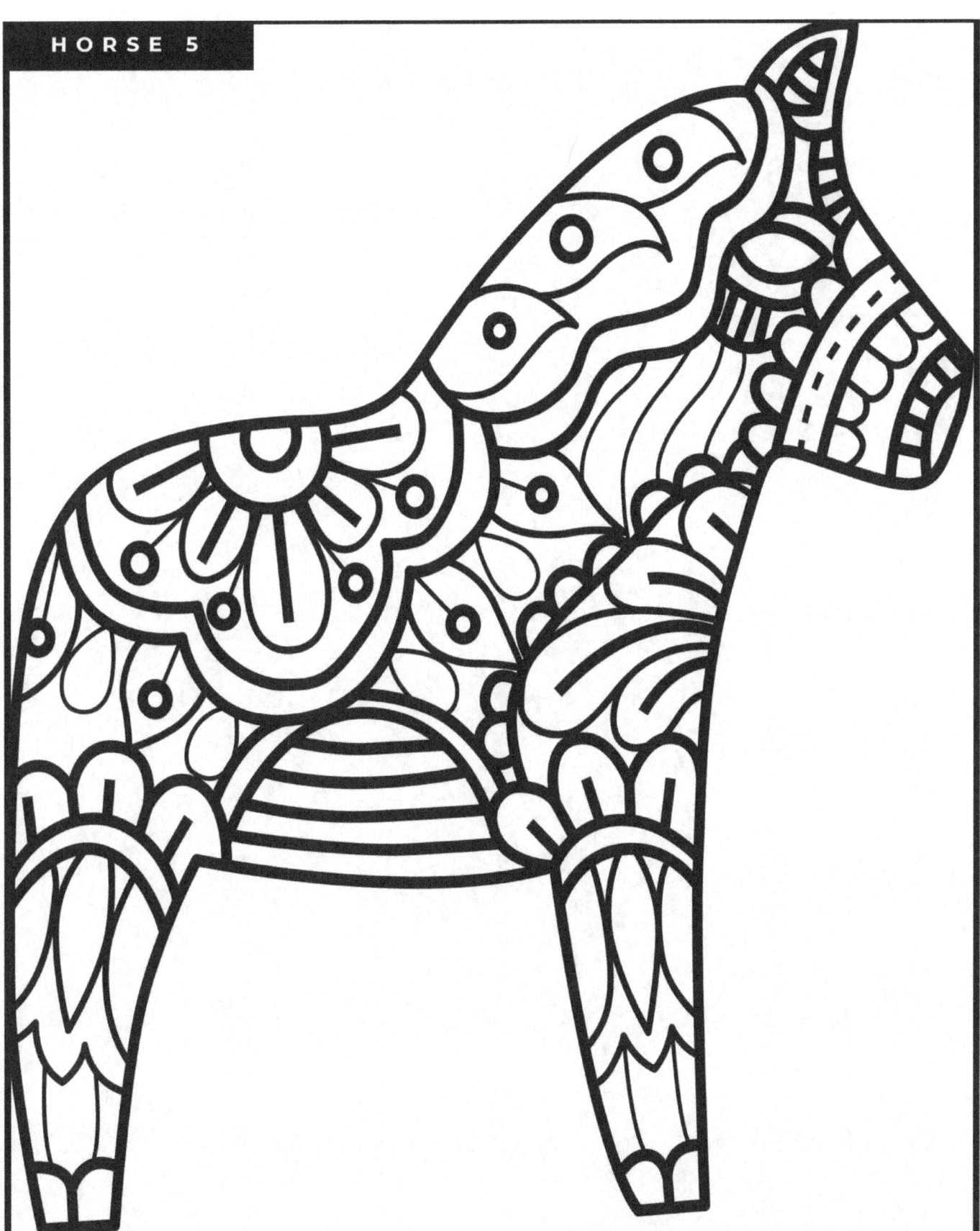

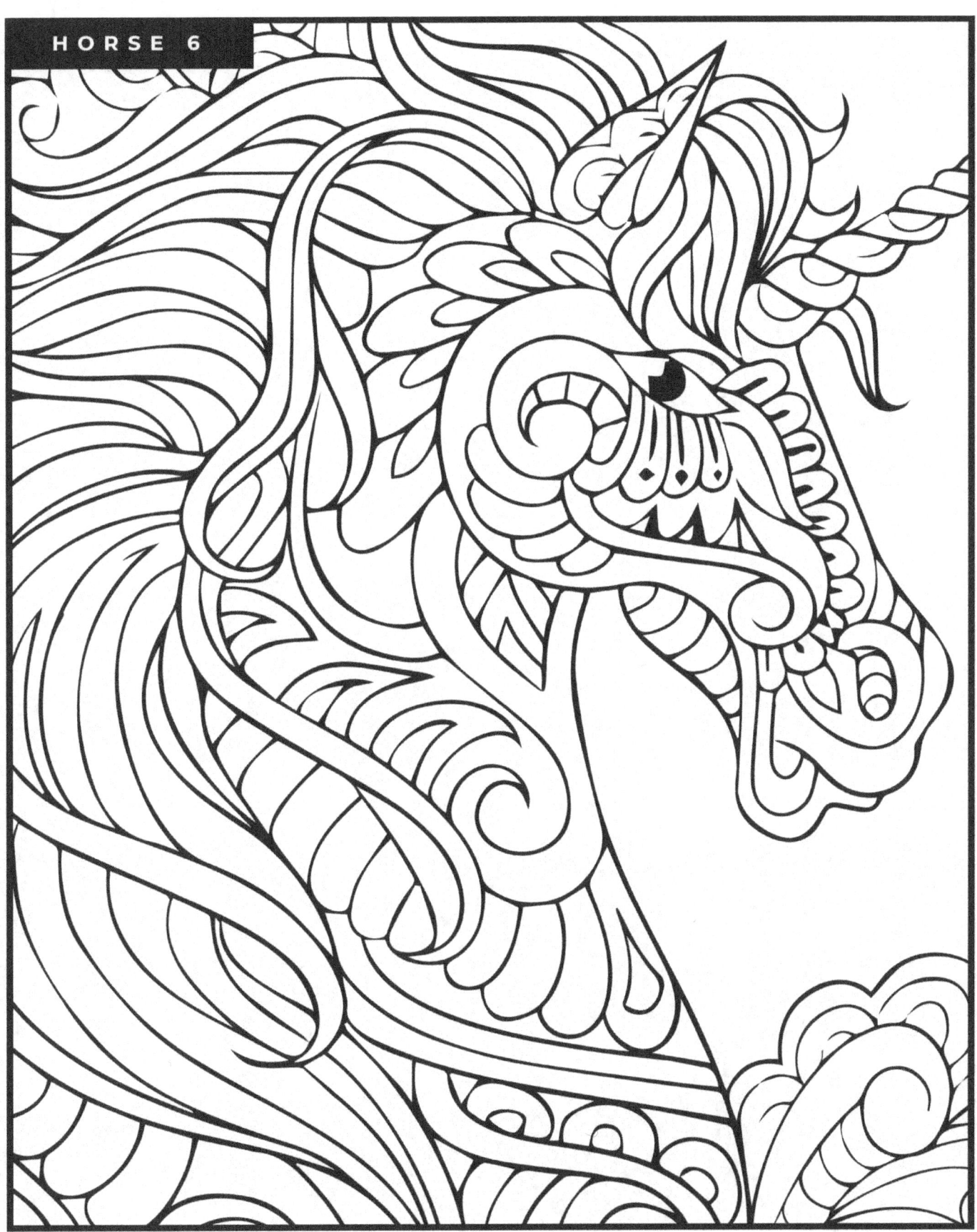

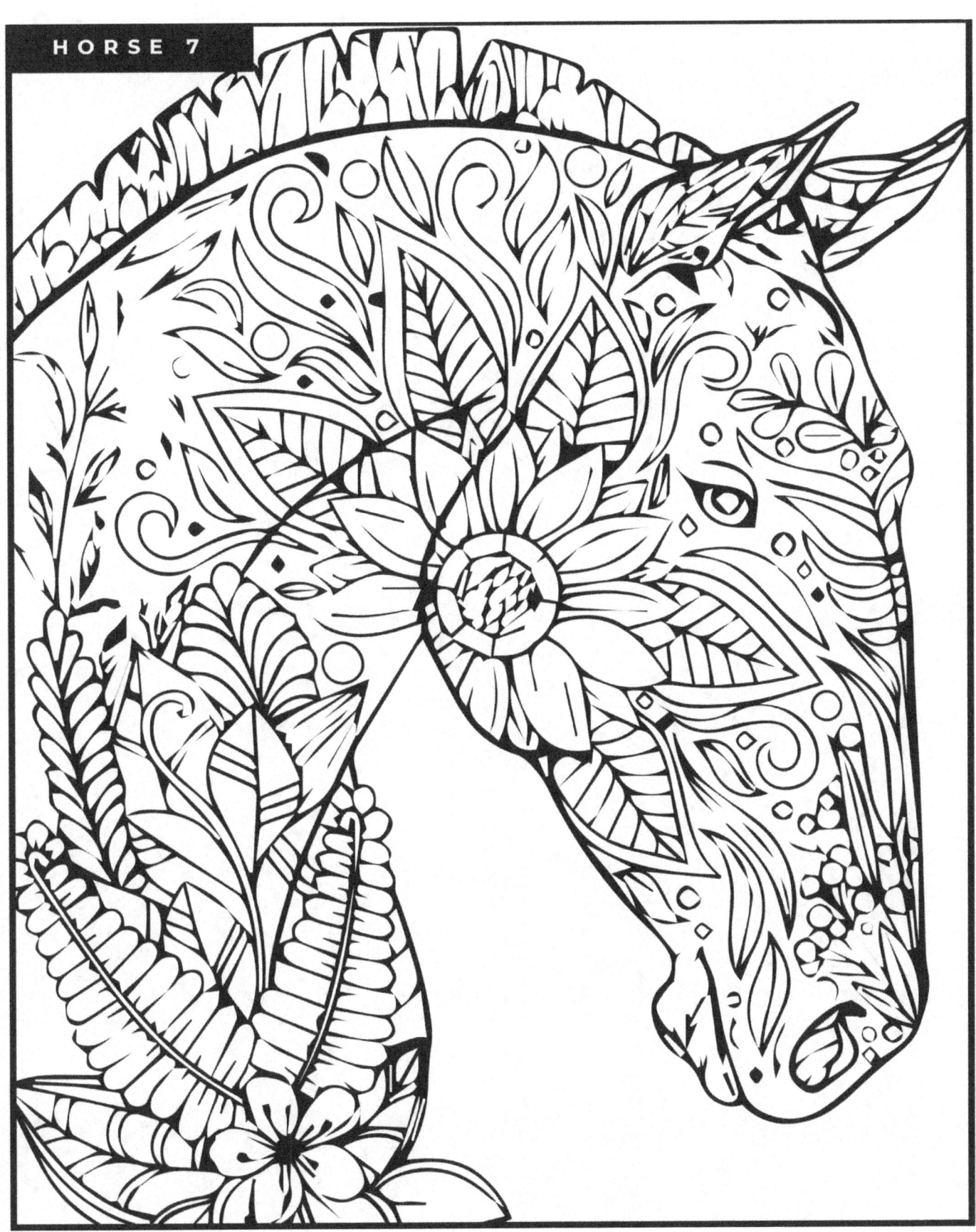

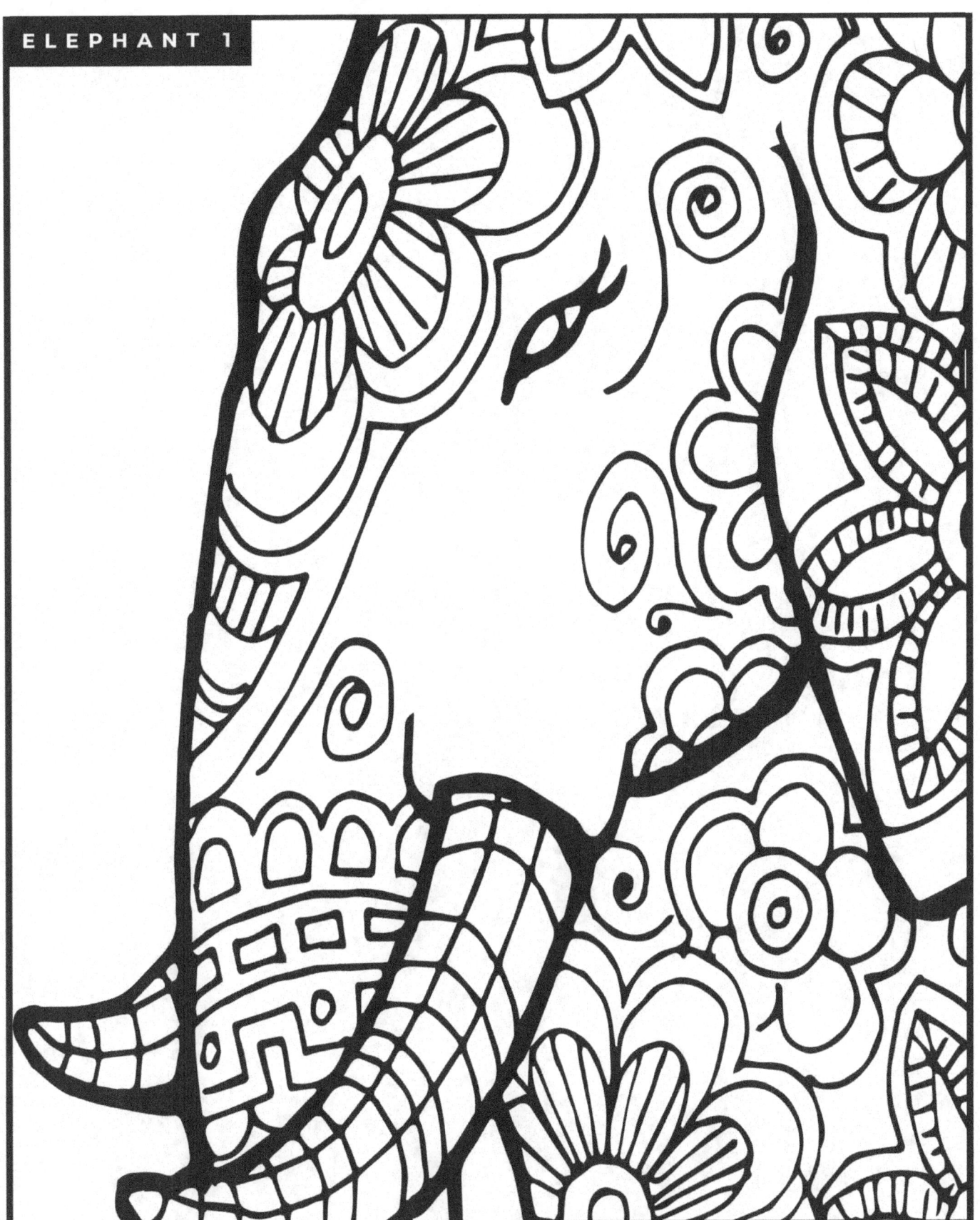

ELEPHANT 2

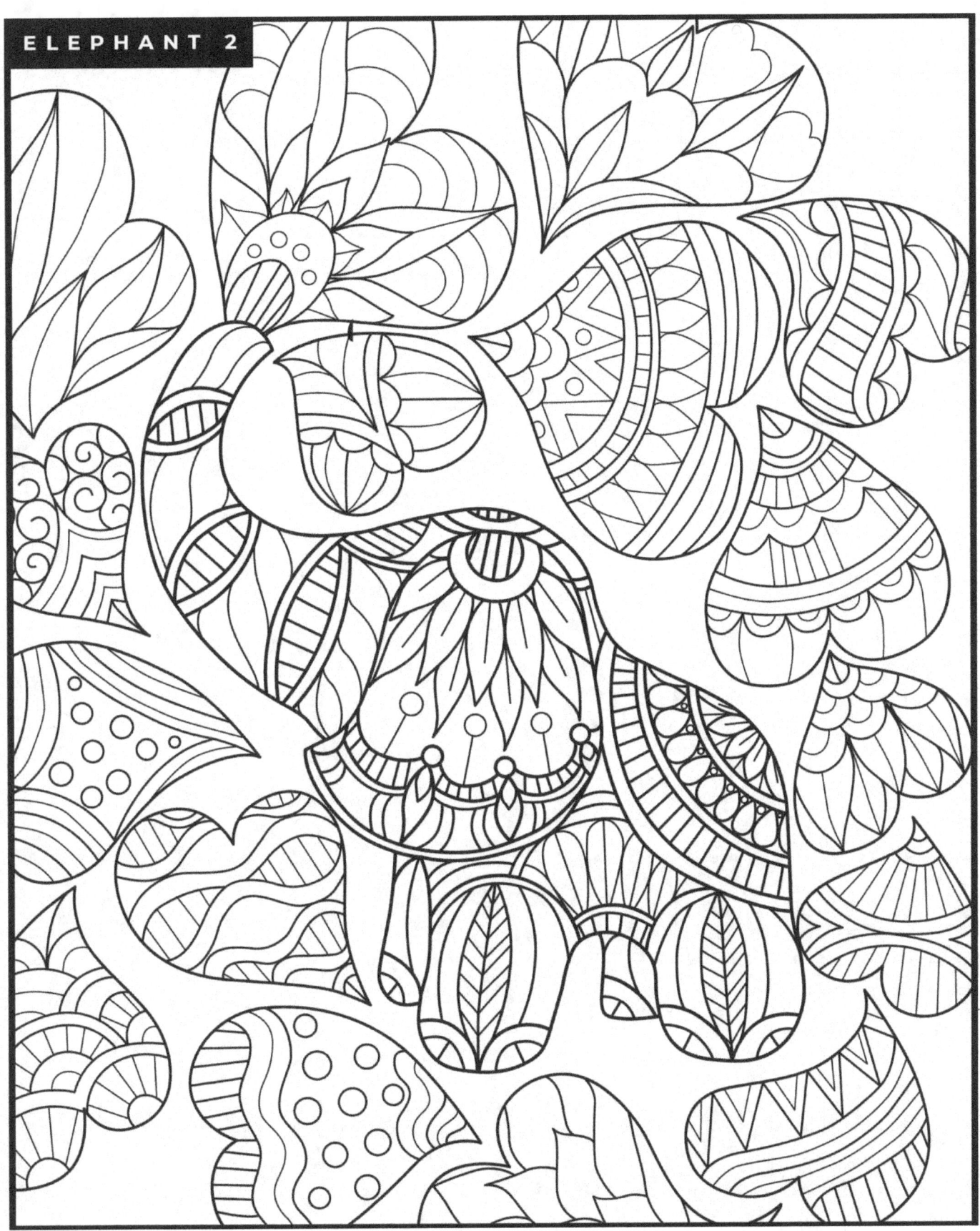

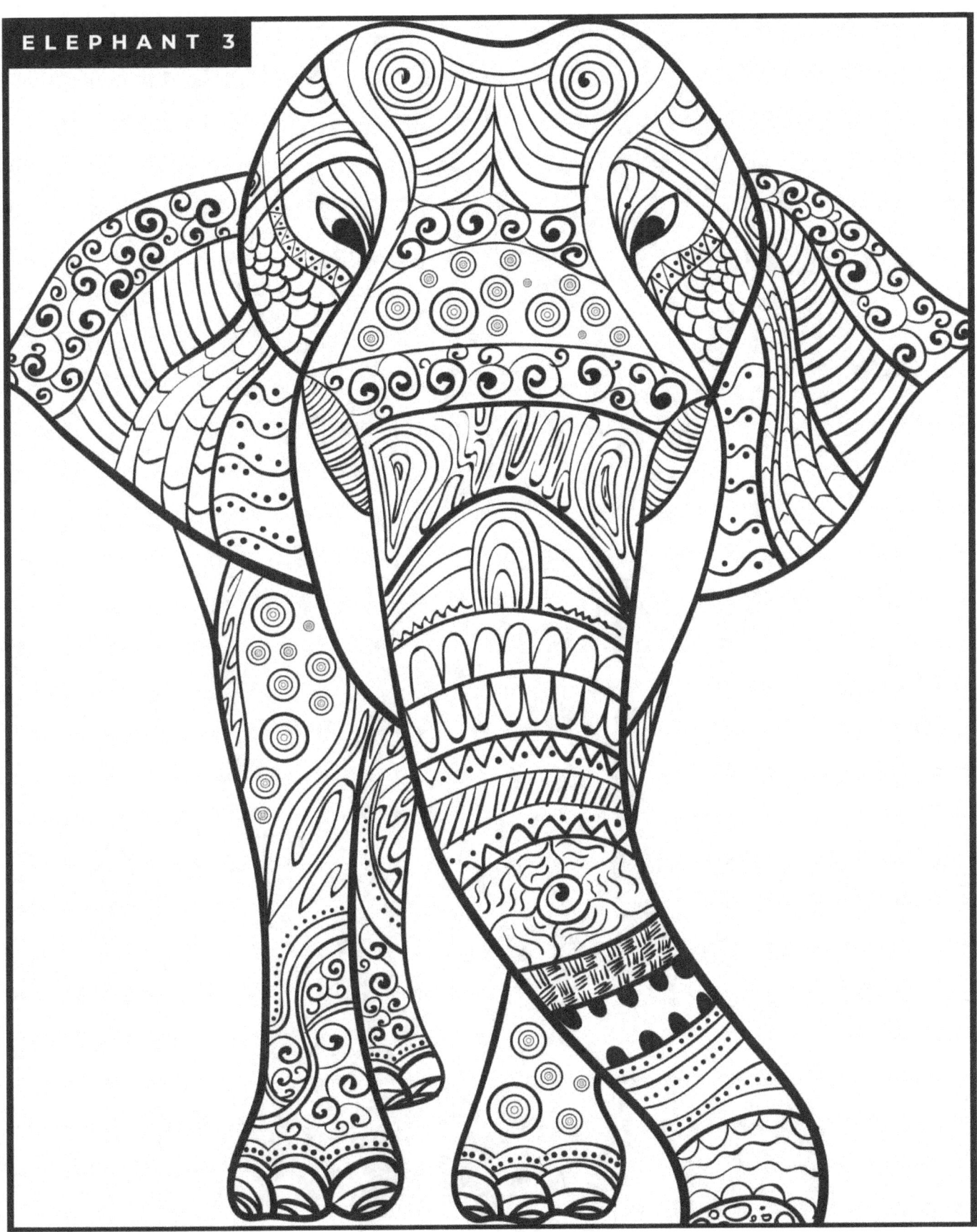

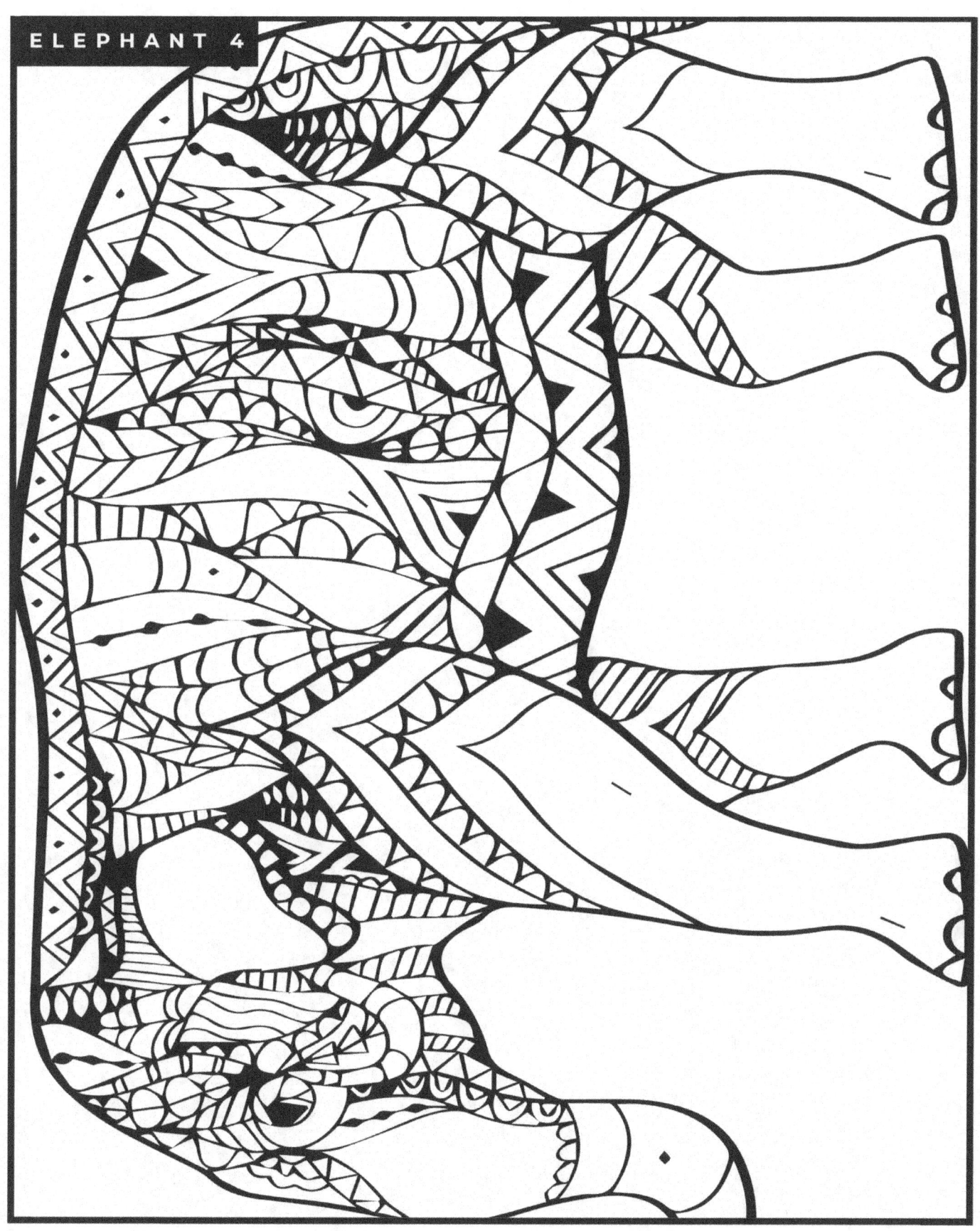

ELEPHANT 4

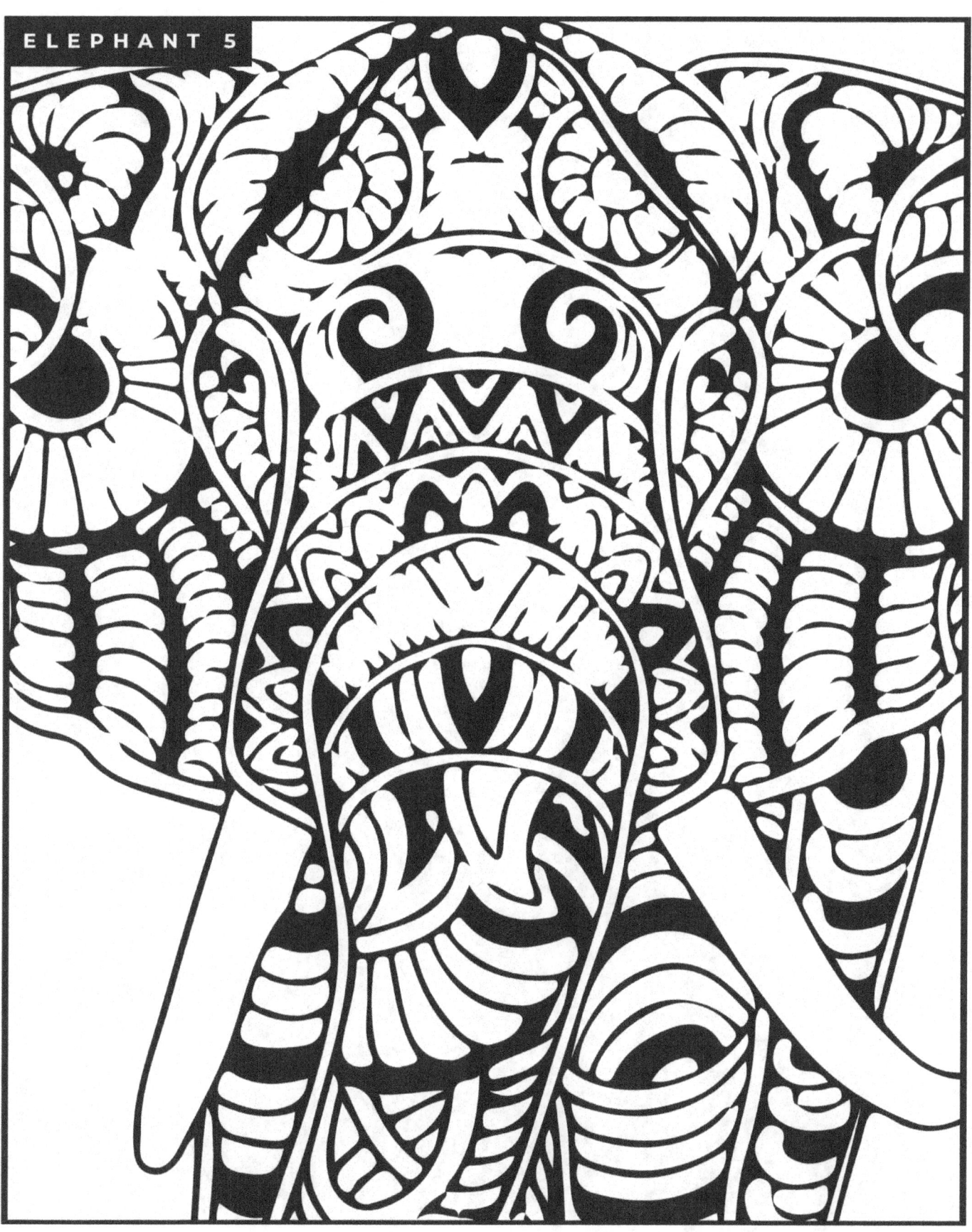

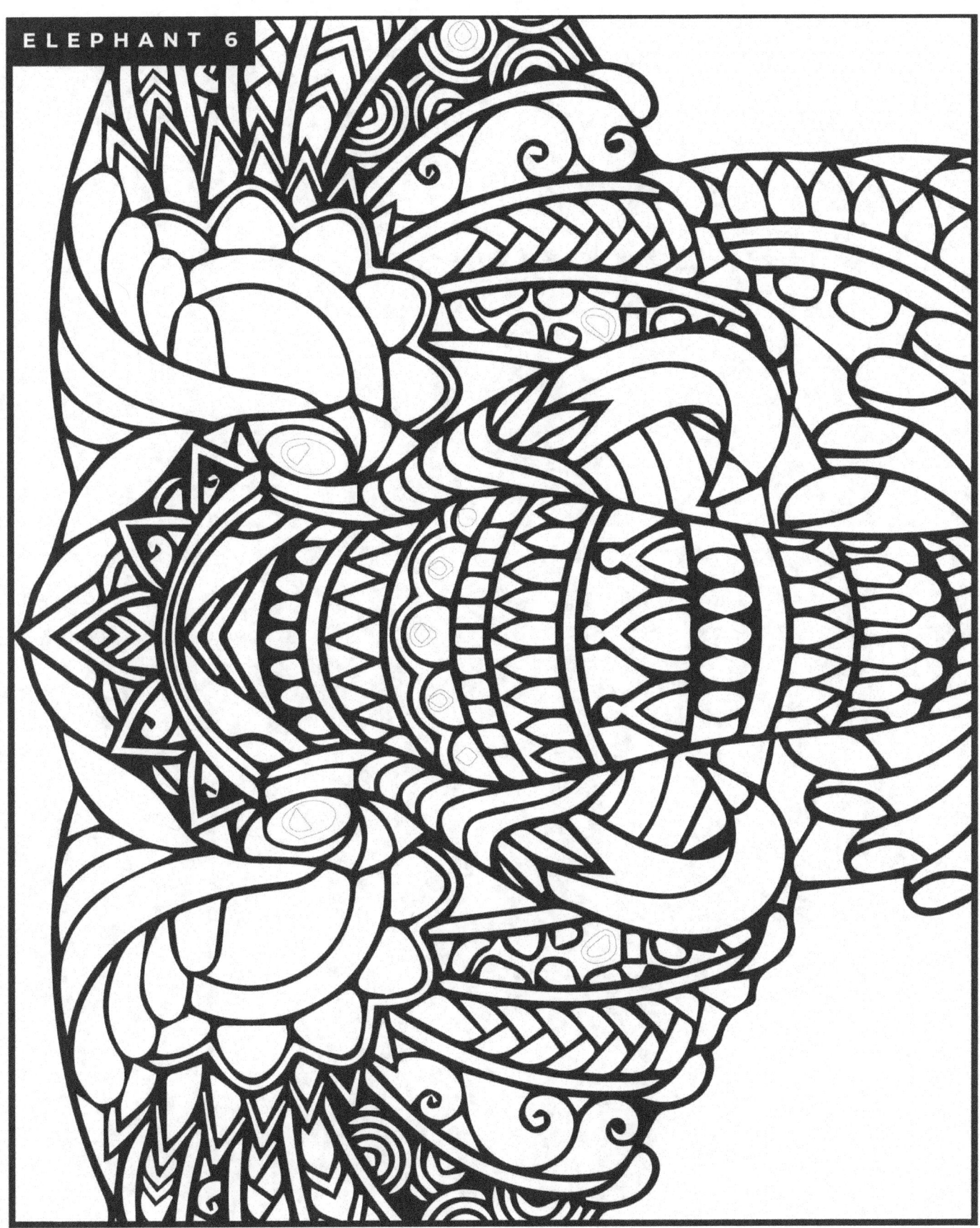

# Minerva P.S. & Co

Minerva Publishing Services and Company was established in 2016. The company was founded by David Marino, an Ecuadorian American who immigrated to the USA in 1999. Minerva is a publication company designed to educate readers on science, physical/mental health, and technology/gaming. Our focus entails disease prevention, nutrition science, and cell biology regarding topics such as autophagy. Our mission is beyond books. We are a proud supporter of Doctors Without Borders. Our book sales help the wonderful staff treat patients all around the world. Through our donations, we can provide chlorination equipment, surgical instruments, blood transfusions, and supplies to build emergency centers for families in need. The sole purpose of Minerva in the future is to provide free health care in the USA and third world countries. Our dedicated readers will help us broaden, mature, and generate worldwide recognition to make everything possible. Since, we live in a social media driven society. It would be helpful if you follow our social media accounts for more helpful tips and entertainment.

**Social Media Accounts:**

Instagram: Minervapsco

Twitter: Minerva_PS_Co

Facebook: Minervapsco

Email: minervapsco.books@gmail.com

# FAQ

**Q: What is Minerva most known for?**

A: Back in 2016, I wrote all my books from scratch and ended up releasing a book on Fortnite that caught the public's attention. That book ended up competing against J.K. Rowling for best seller in Amazon fantasy fiction. On top of that, Minerva has released multiple best sellers in the ketogenic diet and intermittent fasting.

**Q: When will Minerva expand to other products other than books?**

A: We are currently negotiating deals overseas for our first ATM. When our revenue is consistent every month, around 100 published books, we will consider physical products and merchandise.

**Q: How long does it take to research a topic and publish the book on Amazon?**

A: It takes around six months of keyword research and actively seeking new research on biological processes. From start to finish, it may take 10-12 months for a book to be on the shelves.

www.ingramcontent.com/pod-product-compliance
Lightning Source LLC
Chambersburg PA
CBHW081433220526
45466CB00008B/2365